Thomas Wolfe and
the Glass of Time

Thomas Wolfe and the Glass of Time

edited by Paschal Reeves

University of Georgia Press
Athens

Library of Congress Catalog Card Number: 75-156037
Standard Book Number: 8203-0258-9

The University of Georgia Press, Athens 30601

Printed in the United States of America
by The TJM Corporation
Baton Rouge, Louisiana 70821

To Arlin Turner

οὐδὲν ὠφελιμώτερον ἦν τοῦ Σωκράτει συνεῖναι, καὶ μετ᾽ ἐκείνου διατρίβειν ὁπουοῦν καὶ ἐν ὁτῳοῦν πράγματι.

Xenophon, *Memorabilia*, iv, i, i

Contents

Foreword

The University of Georgia is pleased to publish the proceedings of this symposium concerned with the works of Thomas Wolfe. It is fitting that an author from our neighboring state of North Carolina should be the subject of a convocation attended by professors and graduate students from Florida, Georgia, Tennessee, South Carolina, and Wolfe's own native state.

I take special pleasure in this volume since Wolfe has become to me a friend met through another friend. Paschal Reeves, with whom I work on a day-by-day basis in administrative matters, has the ability to infect all of those around him with his own interest and lively knowledge of this remarkable author. Few university presidents, especially those with backgrounds in biological sciences, have had the privilege of trying to help decipher Wolfe's notes or of approaching the personal relationship to an author that comes through an association with an outstanding scholar who has spent a large part of his life in the pursuit of deeper understanding of a literary figure.

I wish to commend the South Atlantic Graduate English Cooperative Agreement and to point it out as a fine example of the kind of regional cooperation that contributes substantially not only to the quality of graduate instruction but also to the general pursuit of excellence in the humanities. The University of Georgia is proud to participate in this program with sister institutions in the Southeast. These institutions include Emory University, Florida State University, the University of Florida, the University of North Carolina, the University of South Carolina, the University of Tennessee, and Vanderbilt University.

We look forward to a continuing productive relationship through this cooperative agreement and hope that the symposium on Thomas Wolfe is only one of many scholarly works that will result.

Fred C. Davison

The University of Georgia
Athens, Georgia
January 15, 1971

Preface

When Thomas Wolfe's first book appeared in 1929 the reviewer for the *New York Times* declared of *Look Homeward, Angel*: "Assuredly, this is a book to be savored slowly and reread, and the final decision upon it, in all probability, rests with another generation than ours." This perceptive observation of Margaret Wallace could well be extended to apply to all of Wolfe's work. Although his books have been, and still are, widely read and he has long since become firmly established as a major American author, his exact position is yet disputed and controversy continues to swirl about his big books. While three decades after his death is still too soon to attempt a final decision, nevertheless it is an appropriate time to make a reassessment. Any revaluation of Wolfe's position, however, must of necessity be a critical reappraisal, since his work has never wavered in its popular appeal.

Critical confusion about Wolfe's work has resulted largely from two basic reasons, his unorthodox manner and the way in which his work achieved publication. He has indeed, as C. Hugh Holman has noted, put unwary critics to the severest test of any American writer since Whitman. His autobiographical prose fiction defies any attempt to categorize it with the conventional critical vocabulary, and he fits into none of the accepted molds.

Though he received the best formal education of all his important contemporaries, he was, as William Faulkner observed, "willing to throw away style, coherence, all the rules of preciseness, to try to put all the experience of the human heart on the head of a pin." And in addition to his freedom from the traditional restraints upon the novelist, he is unique in that half of his total work was published posthumously from an unfinished manuscript. The uncertainty about the role played by a sympathetic but not unerring editor in shaping the posthumous books for the press has also contributed to the general confusion. Wolfe, like Edgar Allan Poe and Walt Whitman, became a legend during his own lifetime and, like theirs, his literary reputation has suffered the distortion and exaggeration of legend, half-truth, anecdote, and fabrication masquerading as fact.

Over the years Wolfe has attracted the attention of many able scholars and a large body of sound criticism has gradually evolved. In 1953 Richard Walser collected a representative portion of the best work done on Wolfe and published the collection as *The Enigma of Thomas Wolfe*. This important book served to emphasize the diversity of opinion about Wolfe and to point out essential work that needed to be done. One of the fundamental needs of Wolfe scholarship, however, was not met until 1962 when Richard S. Kennedy published *The Window of Memory: The Literary Career of Thomas Wolfe*. This comprehensive study of the mind and art of Wolfe is based on a thorough examination of the voluminous materials in the William B. Wisdom Collection in the Harvard Library, and it has proved to be a milestone in understanding Wolfe. With the growing solid body of scholarship it became obvious that one of the important Wolfe documents needed to be redone, and in 1968 C. Hugh Holman (who had already edited Wolfe's *Short Novels*) with Sue Fields Ross brought out *The Letters of*

Thomas Wolfe to his Mother newly edited from the original manuscripts. Through the labors of these scholars and others Wolfe's work is being brought into proper perspective and is being given the necessary basis for sound judgment.

When the University of Georgia decided to devote its first SAGE symposium (held on April 10-12, 1969) to Thomas Wolfe it invited these three scholars to read papers on important but unresolved questions and to join in discussion of related matters that need resolution or clarification. It also invited Fred W. Wolfe, brother of the novelist and sole survivor of his immediate family, to share his intimate memories; Ladell Payne of Claremont Men's College, author of *Thomas Wolfe* in the Southern Writers Series, to lead a discussion on the importance of Wolfe's dramatic apprenticeship on his fiction; and the director of the symposium to lead the final discussion on trends in Wolfe scholarship. In addition to the usual invitation to other SAGE institutions, an open invitation was extended to every interested person and many able students of Wolfe responded and attended the sessions of the symposium and participated in the stimulating and informative discussions. The high quality and lasting worth of the papers read and the illumination and importance of the ensuing discussions has led the University of Georgia to make the proceedings of the symposium available to a wider audience.

The formal papers were presented from manuscript and are published as their authors submitted them. The banquet speech of Mr. Fred Wolfe and all the discussions were recorded and edited from transcription made from the tapes. Any errors in the transcription are the fault of the editor and not of the speaker, since the tapes were at some points not as clear as one might wish; the editor, however, has made every reasonable effort to render an accurate record except for deletions necessary to meet space requirements. The speakers are identified by last name only with a single exception; Professor George M. Reeves, Jr., of the University of South Carolina is identified by his given name to distinguish his remarks from those of the editor of this volume. Full identity of the speakers may be determined by consulting Appendix A. This list consists only of those who registered or participated in the discussion; unfortunately there is no record of the many who attended the sessions of the symposium but did not register or join in the taped discussion.

The symposium was sponsored by the Department of English (Robert H. West, head) and the College of Arts and Sciences (H. Boyd McWhorter, dean). The presentation of Wolfe's one-act play "Gentlemen of the Press," which preceded the discussion led by Mr. Payne, was given by the Readers Theatre of the Department of Drama and Theatre. Mrs. Faye E. Head directed the play and the actors were William Wolak, Stanley Longman, Gerald Kahan, and Jack Beasley. The invited guests were presented complimentary banquet tickets through the courtesy of the Citizens and Southern National Bank of Athens (Hudson D. Whitley, vice president). To all of these we are grateful for their help in making the symposium a success.

The letter from Thomas Wolfe to Mrs. William E. Dodd, heretofore unpublished, is printed with the kind permission of Paul Gitlin, administrator of the Estate of Thomas Wolfe. We wish to thank John C. Broderick, assistant chief, Manuscript Division, Library of Congress, for locating the letter.

I am also grateful to the staff of the University of Georgia Press for their able assistance in bringing this work to fruition. In the preparation of the manuscript for the press I have been greatly aided by Mrs. Connie Smith.

Paschal Reeves

Richard S. Kennedy

Thomas Wolfe's Fiction: The Question of Genre

> I must create a System or be enslav'd by another Man's.
> I will not Reason & Compare; my business is to create.
> —William Blake, *Jerusalem*

Some years ago, after I had finished writing a book on Thomas Wolfe's literary career, I finally found time to read through Northrop Frye's *Anatomy of Criticism,* a work I had hitherto known only through the reading of scattered chunks. I realized then that many of the critical problems of Wolfe's fiction and the whole question of his critical reception and of his subsequent literary reputation lay in the area of genre. Frye's discussion of "confession" and of "anatomy" opened the possibilities for a new view of Wolfe's work.[1] When I began to consider the problem with more care, however, I still found difficulties. Wolfe's fiction is an amazing mixture and none of his longer works fit easily into categories, even into ones as wide and welcoming as those which Frye established. I saw that Wolfe's works were like novels in that they dealt with human relationships in a recognizable and complex society. Yet, as in romances, his characters were sometimes drawn to stylized heroic scale and his narratives even included supernatural episodes, such as the conversation with the ghost which concludes *Look Homeward, Angel* or the

1. "Specific Continuous Forms (Prose Fiction)," *Anatomy of Criticism* (Princeton, 1957), pp. 303-314.

dialogue with the image in the mirror which concludes *The Web and the Rock.* In another way his works were more like those that Frye labeled confessions because they were fictional autobiography. Yet Wolfe's work also resembled the anatomy because of his characteristic habit of encyclopedic compilation and because of his unusual mixture of styles.

Frye has deliberately made his scheme very loose, and in order to avoid overly strict applications, he declared that "exclusive concentration in one form is rare and that hybrid forms of two or even three in combination will be found." Indeed, in dealing with Joyce's *Ulysses,* he declares that "all four forms are employed in it, all of practically equal importance, and all essential to one another." I was not sure that I could see that kind of proportion and that kind of integration in any of Wolfe's works. Moreover, I recognized that the acceptance of Frye's terminology in 1960 was a pretty uncertain business, nor was I eager to reconsider the critical conclusions of my completed book or to rewrite it, especially since I had been compelled for entirely different reasons to rewrite it once. So I merely added the following words near the end of my book: Wolfe "called his pieces of autobiographical fiction novels. Because literary criticism of prose narrative was (and still is) in a rudimentary stage, Wolfe encountered the charge that he was not writing novels at all, and he was profoundly disturbed by it. If now we turned to Northrop Frye's distinctions among novel, confession, romance, and anatomy, we could perhaps employ a cumbersome, hyphenated term that would apply more accurately than the word novel. But since editorial advice or arrangement pushed Wolfe's work toward the novel and since a set of usable critical terms has not been fully established, we should let the label 'novel' stick."[2]

2. *The Window of Memory: The Literary Career of Thomas Wolfe* (Chapel Hill, 1962), p. 412.

Although I had postponed it, I continued to think about the problem, and I was especially intrigued by the discussion of the form called anatomy. But I eventually concluded that the term anatomy would not do for Wolfe, for the term had been too restrictively defined and too closely tied to a larger design. If anatomy is characterized as "dealing less with people than with mental attitudes," Frye's emphasis on idea and intellectual play would rule out Wolfe's major works. In an admirable amplification of Frye's concept, Philip Stevick has taken a broader view of the term anatomy, for he suspected that it was just a catch-all term for prose works that Frye could not fit into his other categories.[3] Stevick examines some works of this outcast sort to see what features they have in common. He finds not only the tendency to intellectualize, which throws all utopias into this bin, but also a tendency to run counter—both in theme and form—to established norms. Even with Stevick's amplification, the term anatomy will not accommodate Wolfe for two clear reasons. First, Wolfe seeks the center of the cultural values of his time. There is nothing subversive about him. He builds; he embraces; he does not tear down or reject. Even when he is satirical he is more likely to criticize those who deviate from traditional ways and beliefs rather than those who are too orthodox. The second reason: when Wolfe bursts the bounds of form he does not do so in order to overturn established forms—none of his works could be called an anti-novel. What he tries to do, rather, is to cram into his work materials that are too large, too unwieldy, or too unusual for the traditional novel and what is more, he tries to stuff too many of them in.

Frye's theory of genre is only a scheme imposed upon literary works in order to organize thought and discussion about them, and the chief value of his theory of fictional

3. "Novel and Anatomy: Notes Toward an Amplification of Frye," *Criticism*, X (1968), 153-165.

genre is in providing perspective on the great variety of
fictional works and warning us not to judge all fiction
according to the standards of the realistic novel. When
Frye is vague and evasive with literary definitions, there
is virtue in his not being absolute, for literary theories are
best when they are not exact and demanding. We sometimes forget that we are dealing with art and not with
science. Thus Robert Scholes, in his recent article on genre
in fiction,[4] has the wisdom to point out that a critic must
be aware of genre before making literary judgments, but
then he goes on into troubled theorizing: he is too exact
and he re-uses old terms in new and arbitrary ways.

I have come to be wary of criticism of this sort, for
most genre criticism works from the outside. The genre
critic approaches literary phenomena with bags and boxes
of distinctive shapes and sizes, and he tries, then, like a
packer from United Van Lines, to see which items fit, and
how well, into the containers he has supplied. Analytical
criticism, quite the opposite, works from the inside. Even
when dealing with questions of genre, the analytical critic
examines what elements constitute the work and make it
what it is. If he finds no box or barrel which can contain
the work satisfactorily, he tries to build one, using what
knowledge he has about well known and serviceable containers. This is what has to be done, it seems to me,
whenever a critic encounters an unusual literary work.
Many critics were simply unable to deal with such works
as *The Waste Land* and *Ulysses* when they first appeared.
Critics are more practiced now and they do better with
such challenges as Nabokov's *Pale Fire* or Barth's *The
Floating Opera*.

This special critical treatment has never been applied
to Wolfe's fiction, although responses to it have con-

4. "Towards a Poetics of Fiction: An Approach Through Genre,"
Novel, II (1969), 101-111.

tinually reflected generic problems. Three decades ago reviewers had difficulty assessing his fictional work because they had in their heads a certain picture of the novel as a form. Even so astute a critic as Robert Penn Warren felt *Of Time and the River* was not a proper novel "but only a series of notes from which a great novel might be written."[5] Later some critics who had more time for consideration of literary problems than the reviewers did still produced responses which showed their limitations whenever the techniques of analytical criticism were not applied empirically enough. Mark Schorer used Wolfe as one of his examples of failure in technique because Wolfe's works did not fulfill his generic expectations: they were, he said, not novelistic enough.[6]

Let us approach Wolfe's work empirically to inquire about what elements make it up, about its structural principles, about the traditions it reflects, about its likeness and unlikeness to other works, about its characteristic features that seem to place it in one category or another, and finally to ask what evaluative criteria can be properly applied to works like Wolfe's which tend to be *sui generis*. To hold the paper within tolerable limits I am going to devote most of my remarks to Wolfe's middle period, from 1930 to 1935.

Let me go directly to a distinctive feature of Wolfe as

5. "A Note on the Hamlet of Thomas Wolfe," *American Review,* V (1935), 191-208, reprinted in Richard Walser, ed., *The Enigma of Thomas Wolfe* (Cambridge, Mass., 1953), pp. 120-132.

6. "Technique as Discovery," *Hudson Review,* I (1948), 67-87. This same shortsightedness troubled Wolfe's editors Maxwell Perkins and Edward Aswell in their handling of his work. Perkins advised Wolfe not to publish his second novel "K 19" because it did not conform to the usual ways of a novel. Aswell cut out much of Wolfe's experimenting with fictional techniques, and he was so uneasy about Wolfe's linguistic exuberance that he felt Wolfe's best writing was to be found in the *You Can't Go Home Again* section of his last manuscript.

a writer, the structural principle he followed in developing his fictional products. When we examine the way Wolfe worked, from the inception of *Look Homeward, Angel* until the end of his career, we find that he let his mind follow associations from one thought to the next, a method of development that is common to lyric poetry rather than prose narrative. Arnold's "Dover Beach," for example, moves from a view of a moonlit seascape, to a thought of the ebb and flow of the sea, to a memory of Sophocles' use of that image to stand for human misery, to an image of ebb tide suggesting the decline of religious faith, to a plea that the beloved one pledge the speaker her personal faith because of the moral chaos of modern life, which is like a confused battle. It is a splendid demonstration of what the shifts and developments of associative thought can bring about. Even when a poet projects his feeling upon a character and a setting in a lyric poem, this associative principle is the common method of development. In Edwin Arlington Robinson's "The Man Against the Sky" the speaker sees a human figure mount a hill at sunset and then disappear down the dark opposite side. But the poem then moves through three-hundred lines of meditation on what kind of a man he was and what his future life was going to be, until the symbolic suggestion has built up an awareness that the meditation is really about mankind pacing out its future and considering whether that future life is worth living.

Fictional works which employ this associative principle I am going to call lyric fiction. I might digress to say that Wolfe is not unique among his contemporaries in having employed this method. It was a natural development in fictional technique as the modern fiction writers began to turn inward, and it became one of the common means of breaking with Victorian and Edwardian traditions in fiction. Joyce, Virginia Woolf, and Proust all used it skillfully in the 1920s. Beckett, Bellow, and Pyncheon are still using it in the 1960s.

The associative principle began to operate as soon as Wolfe started the outline for his first book. He filled two good-sized writing tablets full of notes strung along in phrases as his mind jumped from one thought to another. For example, in the early pages we find:

> 1904 St. Louis—the Fair—I remember having to change and go up a flight of stairs at Cincinnatti—The house we lived in—the two little boys who rode tricycles up and down before the house—a large board fence around the house—the back yard—the fierce sun—the two cots which were there for airing—I eat a peach on which there is a fly—swallow the fly—Fred howls with laughter—I become sick and vomit—The Inside Inn—Grover worked there. Grover and the pears. The ride with Effie through the rain before the Cascades. "Force."[7] Mr. Lyerly and mama.
> The period of Grover's sickness. His death. That night—"the cooling board" Mable. Papa's arrival from home. The ride home. The stairs at Cincinnatti. Coming up the river from Knoxville[.] Home—the cry of Mrs. Perkinson—Ashville—the great dignity and authority of the familiar—"only one Asheville." Nora Israel in the parlour. The rest (Dear Brutus) is silence (Ben and Grover—what are twins like—Did Ben carry this strange doom with him—a brooding fatality, until his death.[)] The coffin in the parlour—we had just arrived. How did it get there? Had we waited at the station?
> 1905-1906—Max Israel—Charley Perkinson—the fire department—Christmas—the pony—the first compositions—Sept. 1906—I go off to school.[8]

As he wrote his book, he would cross out those notations he used, thus *Look Homeward, Angel* as we have it now moves by means of these associative leaps. The association of ideas may provide a means of movement but it does not offer good opportunity for control. Lyric poems, we note, are usually short. If they are long, they tend to fall into a series of short units which make up the whole

7. This has reference to some material that was cut out of *Look Homeward, Angel*. Eugene, as a tiny little boy, has an exquisite enjoyment of food, including a breakfast cereal called "Force."

8. Autobiographical Outline in the Harvard College Library 46AM-7(25).

as in Whitman's *Song of Myself* or Tennyson's *In Memoriam*. Or perhaps the poet may use an autobiographical time scheme to impose control on his material. Thus Wordsworth in *The Prelude* rehearses the development of his sensibilities over the years. Wolfe used the autobiographical device for a guide line to hold onto, and it became the one he turned to most naturally for the rest of his life. Therefore, in spite of its lyric method, *Look Homeward, Angel* falls in the category of the *Bildungsroman* very well, for the defining characteristic of the *Bildungsroman* is the movement of the central character through the struggles of growing up until he reaches maturity, a point at which he has sufficient understanding of life to bring his career somewhat under control, free from the mistakes of the past.[9]

But *Look Homeward, Angel* is an unusual example of this sub-category of prose fiction. Most *Bildungsromans* begin with a focus on the central character's raising some question of his identity, like Dickens' Pip in *Great Expectations*: "My father's name being Pirrip, and my Christian name Philip, my infant tongue could make of both names nothing longer or more explicit than Pip. So, I called myself Pip, and came to be called Pip." Or they begin with the parentage as in Butler's *The Way of All Flesh*, which starts with a look at old Mr. Pontifex, or as in Meredith's *The Ordeal of Richard Feverel*, which takes a first look at Sir Austin Feverel and his book of aphorisms. But *Look Homeward, Angel* begins with an incantation: "... a stone, a leaf, an unfound door ... of a stone, a leaf, a door. And of all the forgotten faces." If we do not count that as the beginning, but take the opening of chapter one, we still do not begin with a character or an ancestor but with the cosmos and a meditation on the miracle of chance.

9. For a full discussion of Wolfe and the *Bildungsroman*, see my "*Look Homeward, Angel* as a Novel of Development," *South Atlantic Quarterly*, LXIII (1964), 218-226.

Another means besides autobiography for imposing an order on a long lyric piece is the use of myth. This is what Eliot tried to do for *The Waste Land* and what Joyce really did use to hold together the individual sections of *Ulysses*.[10] Wolfe employed myth very effectively in *Look Homeward, Angel*—two myths in fact, the Platonic myth of pre-existence and the naturalistic myth of the universe governed by chance. In spite of these patterns *Look Homeward, Angel* does not have a plot in the way a novel does. It does not move from initial situation by means of probable incidents that arise out of the inter-relationship of the characters. It follows the method of a long lyric poem.

When Wolfe prepared to write a second long work, he determined not to use the autobiographical time-scheme for control because too many acquaintances, editorial friends, and reviewers had implied that this was the mark of an apprentice. But as soon as he tried out other devices to govern his material, he got into terrible trouble. He held to myth, however, attempting to use the story of Antaeus and Heracles, but it was inadequate for his needs. He flailed about, writing meditations on time, home, love, ancestry. He worked on sequences about Americans in Europe, about a train ride, about Aline Bernstein's child-hood, about her father, about a teacher he had known at New York University, and about the childhood of a monkey-like boy who dreamed of running away with a circus.[11] But he could not sustain anything for very long. Only when he began veering back toward the autobio-graphical scheme did he feel secure.

At last, when he was forced to publish something, he

10. See Eliot's discussion of this technique "*Ulysses*, Order, and Myth," reprinted from *The Dial* (1923) in *Criticism: The Foundations of Modern Literary Judgment*, ed. Mark Schorer et al. (New York, 1948).

11. See *The Notebooks of Thomas Wolfe*, ed. Richard S. Kennedy and Paschal Reeves (Chapel Hill, 1970), pp. 449-535.

produced short works suitable for periodical publication, and he employed autobiography (with a first-person narrator) to help hold those works together, and he began to try out some new devices within the autobiographical framework. "The Portrait of Bascom Hawke," his novella-length piece published in 1932, makes use of a character sketch interwoven with autobiographical reminiscence. "As for plot," he wrote to Maxwell Perkins, "there's not any, but there's an idea which I believe is pretty plain —I've always wanted to say something about *old men* and *young men,* and that's what I've tried to do here."[12]

The next work, "The Web of Earth" (1932), is Wolfe's most successful grappling with his method of development by association. His speaker, Delia Hawke, begins telling about a mysterious voice she heard saying "Two, two. Twenty, twenty." Soon she has digressed into reminiscences of her childhood and memories of Sherman's troops coming to the farm and anecdotes of her grandparents and uncles and on to a story about two murderers escaped from the town jail. Each piece of the story reminds her of another story, which in turn leads her to another story, until, after several narratives have been introduced, Wolfe turns her around in the middle. She then moves backwards and winds up one narrative after another until she finally has disclosed the birth of her twins and the meaning of the ghostly whisperings. Meanwhile Wolfe has gathered a rich assembly of characters and accumulated symbolic associations around Delia Hawke as an earth mother and around her husband as a Dionysian harvest god.

But he never attempted this symmetrical interweaving of associations again—perhaps because it would have made his publications too much alike, but perhaps also

12. *The Letters of Thomas Wolfe,* ed. Elizabeth Nowell (New York 1956), p. 316.

because the work is so constantly digressive that it is hard to follow.

The next work is more autobiographical but it employs the associative principle in its over-all organization in a new manner. "Death the Proud Brother" (1933) is arranged in a sequence of four reminiscences of death scenes which the narrator has witnessed. Nevertheless, the lyric quality predominates: the work begins with a meditation on night and moves to a consideration of Death, Loneliness, and Sleep, all personified as forces of the night. As the four death scenes are recounted, the narrator focuses not on an action that brought about death, but rather on the impact each death has upon the passing city-dwellers and upon himself. It ends with some pondering of the meaning of Death and an apostrophe to Death, Loneliness, and Sleep. This was a kind of structure Wolfe was to use a number of times thereafter—for example in "The Four Lost Men." When we note how much like the personal essay this piece is, we remember that the personal essay is the prose form most like the short lyric poem. Indeed, it is not surprising that the beginning of the nineteenth century which saw the development of the personal essay in the work of Lamb, De Quincey, and Hazlitt was the same period that saw the high achievement in lyric poetry by Wordsworth, Coleridge, Keats, and Shelley. Both are manifestations of a psychic turning-inward in literary expression. Wolfe's "Death the Proud Brother" with its lyric method is in the same genre as De Quincey's *Confessions of an English Opium Eater.*[13]

13. One should add that during this same year Wolfe was at work on a long piece which dealt with jealousy in love. It focused on the narrator's mad suspicion of his beloved Esther and upon their bitter quarrels. Wolfe called it "A Vision of Death in April," and parts of it later appeared in *The Story of a Novel* and *The Web and the Rock.* Wolfe's model was again De Quincey: both "A Vision of Sudden Death" from *The English Mail Coach* and "The Pains of Opium" from the *Confessions.*

The short fictional works I have been describing all seem to me to have grown and taken their shape rather naturally from the associative method of development. But the next work seems to have been more consciously constructed. "The Train and the City" is a short piece of fiction which follows the archetypal pattern of the Journey and Arrival of the Provincial in the City. We might say that Wolfe adopted myth again for structural unity. Since this attempt was for a short work only, he seems to have had success. But within that pattern are found four different organizational devices by which Wolfe exercises control over his lyric development. Each of them was to become an important means by which Wolfe learned to handle short units of his longer works. The first is the journey. It is a primitive form of narrative construction. It is just one step beyond the autobiographical scheme. If the autobiographical scheme provides movement in time (this happened, and then this, and then this, and so on), the journey combines movement in time and space (this happened in this place, this happened in the next, and so on). Byron used it in *Childe Harold's Pilgrimage* to organize a series of meditations. Picaresque novelists use the journey to tie together a series of episodes unrelated by probability. In "The Train and the City" the narrator has the adventure of participating in a race between two trains: he watches the engineer, the firemen, the porters, and the passengers in the diner of the passing train; he focuses like a Zen Buddhist in meditation on a vein in the back of an old man's hand and he experiences an unforgettable moment. He arrives, then, in the city to be astounded at the "tribal swarm of faces" and to be awed at the "enfabled rock . . . masted like a ship with its terrific towers"; he is amazed to be able to imagine the city as a living being which speaks with its own voice.[14]

14. "The Train and the City" appeared in *Scribner's Magazine* in May 1933, but it is most easily accessible in its revised version in *Of Time and the River* (New York, 1935), pp. 407-419.

Since this is a very short piece, there is not much of a journey, but it is Wolfe's first published work that makes use of this kind of organization. The previous year Wolfe had worked out a short journey book called "K 19," which Maxwell Perkins persuaded him not to publish. It was about a train journey home to the South with character sketches of various home folk who were passengers and with the narrator's discovery that he no longer felt in harmony with the people at home and their way of life. This narrative pattern is one that Wolfe tried over and over again to get published. He arranged it again in a story entitled "Boom Town," but magazine editors demanded ruinous cuts and changes.[15] We recognize that it finally took shape as George Webber's journey south to Libya Hill in *You Can't Go Home Again.* But it was still just a device for pulling short disparate units together.

Now to return to "The Train and the City": the second organizing device is the catalogue. The young provincial brings a representative American's background of ancestry and experience with him to the city. Wolfe presents it in a Whitmanesque style, a series of statements which employ parallel constructions and accumulations of images in series. The effect is rhythmic pleasure combined with a sense of abundance as the fleeting images of the American scene are ticked off: trains pounding the rails, cities at dawn, towns silent at midnight, the dull red of box cars, empty and lonely on sidings. This sequence is followed by a chant, a series of phrases that sum up the experience of his pioneer forbears settling the wilderness. The voices of the ancestors then speak, and within the catalogue we get a rhythmically-arranged epic boast from these dead warriors and builders, a boast of their vitality, their achievement, and even the superior richness of the earth

---

15. Despite the fact that cuts harmed the work, "Boom Town" was selected by Harry Hansen for the *O. Henry Memorial Award: Prize Stories of 1934* after it had been first published in the *American Mercury* in May 1934.

which holds their buried bodies. This moves into a catalogue specifying and characterizing some of the ancestral
dead and stressing the geographical range of their burial
places, Oregon, Virginia, Pennsylvania, California, Old
Catawba, and the presence of both Yankee and Confederate dead at Chancellorsville and Shiloh. To the effect of
abundance and variety is added the sense of the presence
of the past and the value of historical achievement.

Against the breadth and variety of the American landscape and the American past that he has just set forth,
Wolfe places the modern, populous, seemingly chaotic
density of the City. He brings order into the seeming
chaos by means of his third device, collage. I label it thus
because he has gone to his notebooks, culled out and
revised notes of conversations he had overheard in res-
taurants, railway stations, subways, or on street corners.
Out of all this he constructed his composite Voice of the
City, which exhibits such tones as "pugnacious recollec-
tion," "epic brag," "ladylike refinement," "maternal trib-
ulation," "outraged decency," stupefaction, and finally
friendly and familiar exchange of amenities. Although the
material is satirically handled, the effect is not only increased variety with some high contrast to the dignity of
the ancestral voices but also fascination with the curious
forms that human group behavior can bring into being.

Besides the three devices I spoke of a chant by ancestral voices. Note that it is a group of voices in chorus and
that they are elders who are expressing the wisdom of
their experience. Thus this portion of "The Train and the
City" presents a prose version of the choral ode such as
we find in Greek tragedy. I mention this first in connection with the ancestral voices in order to identify the
generic origin of this literary feature, and I want to turn
back to point out that Wolfe has been long developing
this communal voice which speaks somewhat differently
from the voice of an omniscient narrator. That higher

strain is heard in the proem of *Look Homeward, Angel* and heard again in a few places of special emotional intensity in the book, such as the "Ubi sunt" passage addressed to Laura and in the dirge by the grave of Ben. The narrator falls into the communal "we" rather than other pronoun forms. But this device is not developed into full choral chants until Wolf's middle period. The choral voice had emerged once in "The Portrait of Bascom Hawke" in an answer to Bascom Hawke's inability to communicate about the past and in a response to the young man's vision of the old people who have lost their vitality and cannot speak:

> The dry bones, the bitter dust? The living wilderness, the silent waste? The barren land?
> Have no lips trembled in the wilderness? No eyes sought seaward from the rock's sharp edge for men returning home? Has no pulse beat more hot with love or hate upon the river's edge? Or where the old wheel and the rusted stock lie stogged in desert sand: by the horsehead a woman's skull. No love?
> No lonely footfalls in a million streets, no heart that beats its best and bloodiest cry out against the steel and stone, no aching brain, caught in its iron ring, groping among labyrinthine canyons? Naught in that immense and lonely land but incessant growth and ripeness and pollution, the emptiness of forests and deserts, the unhearted, harsh, and metal jangle of a million tongues, crying the belly cry for bread, or the great cat's snarl for meat and honey? All, then, all? Birth and the twenty thousand days of snarl and jangle—and no love, no love? Was no love crying in the wilderness?
> It was not true. The lovers lay below the lilac bush; the laurel leaves were trembling in the wood.[16]

This is not the voice of the first-person narrator speaking; it is as if the ancestral voices are speaking out and through him so that he becomes a kind of oracle and thus

---

16. *The Short Novels of Thomas Wolfe,* ed. C. Hugh Holman (New York, 1961), p. 70.

a group spokesman. These rhythmic imitations of the choral chants are one more device for organizing material.

Wolfe's next publication in 1933 was "No Door," his most important literary work since *Look Homeward, Angel*. (I am referring to the long version of "No Door" which appeared in the July issue of *Scribner's Magazine*). Here is an example of the other kind of organization that Wolfe came to adopt for his longer works besides the autobiography, the journey, and the personal essay. It is an assembly of several units which have thematic likeness, but little or no narrative connection. I know no literary term to describe it. If it were a musical composition, we could call it a tone poem. Since that is not a suitable term, I suggest we call it a thematic anthology.

"No Door" begins with a proem which introduces themes of contrasting aspects of life: of wandering and return home; of death and the recurrence of life in the cycle of nature; of loneliness and its cure in love. Wolfe then selected several units from the material he had been writing—his alter ego's travels, his meditations, his yearning for a father, and his jealousy of his mistress Esther. He changed his mind several times about what to include, and when he did select four fairly complex units, Perkins made him eliminate one long narrative portion in it.[17] When we look at what we have, we long for more thematic coherence among the assembled units, but we do see a work of lyric fiction which employs several of the subsidiary organizing principles Wolfe had learned how to use.

The first unit is an essay on wealthy people who entertain a writer and exclaim with false envy about his rather

17. Holman has reprinted it in *The Short Novels of Thomas Wolfe*, pp. 159-231, in a version which restores the episode which Perkins cut out of Wolfe's manuscript. For a description of Wolfe's developing this work see *The Window of Memory*, p. 258, n. 26.

grubby experiences in urban living, a device which draws together a series of anecdotes about the people in Brooklyn. The second unit combines two characteristically lyric expositions. One is a meditation on the fury of youth, depicting the young narrator in his attempt to read all the books in the Harvard library and in his zest to embrace all the simultaneous events in the city and to touch the life of all the people there. The other lyric presentation is a choral chant, which develops out of thoughts of home: "October has come again . . . ." A voice like that of the ancestral chorus urges the youth to return home but mingles the urging with images of harvest and autumn color all over America and with a picture of a train roaring southward. Note that, of the two lyric expressions, one is individual, involving human desire; the other, communal, invoking the natural scene and the expanse and variety of the national landscape.

The third unit records, in an essay full of anecdotes, some impressions of October in England. Its lyric quality is intensified by rhythmic, evocative language: "Smoke-gold by day, the numb exultant secrecies of fog, a fog-numb air filled with solemn joy of nameless and impending prophecy, an ancient yellow light, the old smoke-ochre of the morning, never coming to an open brightness —such was October in England that year." The development is similar to the collage of the City Voice, except that it extends beyond impressions of English speech to images of bony limbs and ugly facial features and to memories of tasteless food—nor is there any personification. It is a traveler's account of a way of life, and one sufficiently distinct that he feels excluded from it—it is a door he cannot enter.

The last unit is a summary of Esther's visits to the narrator's garret and an account of the trucking firm and its tough-tongued drivers which the lovers see from their window. It does not fit thematically with the other units except for its concluding portion, which presents another choral ode. Again, the choral speaker is an old man, seen unmoving at his desk in the next building. His solidity, his calm, sorrowful eyes invite the narrator's imagination until he hears a voice "that seemed to have all the earth in it . . . and in it were the blended tongues of all those men who have passed through the heat and fury of the day, and who now lean quietly upon the sills of the evening." It speaks as Ecclesiastes addressing modern urban man—"Life is many days," full of tumult and shifting fashions, but "some things will never change." The piece closes with imagistic assurances that the earth abides forever.

As we see, Wolfe was moving toward the solution of his problem of form that blocked his progress in producing a second book. This thematic anthology with its disjunctive shifts from scene to scene and with its mixture of personal essay, meditation, travelogue, and choral chant attempted to join together a series of visions and responses to modern life. As a total work it failed, for the individual units are not coherently related. But the individual units have their own integrity. It remained now for him, with the encouragement of Maxwell Perkins, to go back to the autobiographical sequence, which could join large numbers of units together and allow the variety of the material to find its own thematic connections.

The result was the publication in 1935 of *Of Time and the River*, preceded by that same proem, "of wandering forever and the earth again. . . . " This book was like nothing else that had ever appeared on the American literary scene—vast in scale, over 900 pages long, in scene ranging up and down the Atlantic coast of America and all over England and France, with more than a hundred characters passing before the observant eye of the narrator, who presents us with a shifting generic mixture. Gone is the first-person narrator, to be replaced by an appropriately omniscient narrator once again, who follows Eugene Gant and turns away when necessary for oratorical apostrophe, bardic chant, or nostalgic essay.

What kind of work can we call it? It has the scope and encyclopedic variety that we associate with the term epic, but it has no consistently developed narrative structure. It has the heightened style and the superhuman central figure we associate with the epic, but it also drops down to the realistic dialogue of the novel and to the descriptive excesses of formal satire. Although it deals with a young man discovering life, it is no mere *Bildungsroman,* for it reflects the national life, and it gives major space to developing formal lyric expressions of the great themes commonly found in the work of major poets.

Let us look closely once again at the first section. The book opens on a scene at the railway station where Eugene Gant's family is bidding him good-bye before he leaves for Boston. The treatment is almost a parody of a nineteenth-century novel—say, one by Henry James or Thomas Hardy.[18] A specific time and place are recorded: "About fifteen years ago, at the end of the second decade of this century, four people were standing together on the platform of the railway station of a town in the hills of Western Catawba." An omniscient narrator proceeds in leisurely fashion to describe the scene—the kind of town, the appearance of the crowd. He approaches the characters with a nineteenth-century novelist's formality and hesitation: "It would have been evident to an observer that of the four people who were standing together at one end of the platform three—the two women and the boy —were connected by relationship of blood." The characters are not named for some time, but rather referred to as "the younger woman," "the mother," "the boy," "the

18. One thinks, for example, of *The Portrait of a Lady* or *Tess of the D'Urbervilles.*

older woman." The names emerge only when they begin to speak to other characters standing by and when extended expository dialogue acquaints the reader with information about Eugene's departure for Harvard, about the father's condition in the hospital, and other family matters. But we discover later that neither the bulk of the dialogue nor the identification of the friends and relatives in this scene points forward to further action or significance in the book. This work which opens like a novel does not continue to develop like a novel.

In the scene, however, there are a few hints of generic deviation from the usual novelistic development: in paragraph two the narrator mentions with authoritative inclusiveness that these people have come together to await the train "an event which has always been of first interest in the lives of all Americans." One also notices exaggeration and stylization in the handling of the characters, especially Eugene, who groans miserably, shouts incoherently, and mutters darkly like a junior-grade King Lear: "Peace, peace, peace, peace, peace. A moment's peace for all of us before we die."[19] We remember too that the section was entitled "Orestes: Flight before Fury" and that it was preceded by the rhythmic haunting proem, "of wandering forever and the earth again." The departure from the conventions of the novel form becomes even more evident after twenty pages when we launch into an essay contrasting the North and the South, beginning as Eugene's train arrives: "It was his train and it had come to take him to the strange and secret heart of the great North that he had never known, but whose austere and lonely image, whose frozen heat and glacial fire and dark stern beauty had blazed in his vision since he was a child. For he had dreamed and hungered for the

19. *Of Time and the River* (Scribners: New York, 1935), pp. 7-8. Further page references will be to this edition and will be placed in parenthesis in the text.

proud unknown North with that wild ecstasy, that intoler-able and wordless joy of longing and desire, which only a Southerner can feel" (pp. 23-24)—and it continues on in descriptive balance and contrast. It may be an essay, but its style places it with what De Quincey has called "the literature of power," and its balanced syntax and its cadence (as it accumulates its phrases in series) place it in the tradition of American platform oratory.

This stylistic intensification continues in the next chapter with the description of what a traveler sees as the train moves across the rugged terrain of the American scene: "The great shapes of the hills, embrowned and glowing with the molten hues of autumn, are all about him: the towering summits, wild and lonely, full of joy and strangeness and their haunting premonitions of on-coming winter soar above him, the gulches, gorges, gaps, and wild ravines, fall sheer and suddenly away with a dizzying steepness, and all the time the great train toils slowly down from the mountain summits with the sinuous turnings of an enormous snake (p. 25)." The traveler on this train might be Byron's Manfred or the poet of Shelley's *Alastor*; it could even be Thomas Gray writing a letter from the Alps: the American landscape is described in that romantic style that we associate with the term pic-turesque, and as the passage continues we are aware that it is suitable for conveying a sense of abundance, variety, and movement combined with strangeness.

This shifts into a choral chant: "Who has seen fury riding in the mountains?" The tone, the images continue to reflect the romantic agony—indeed Wolfe borrows some words from Byron about "the little tenement of bone, blood, marrow, brain, and feeling" and places them very early in this six-paragraph ode to fury before it dis-solves into a memory of his father's vigor on an April morning.

The journey has begun, and this organizing device

holds the rest of the section together. We are aware now that the work is made up of short units that melt one into another by means of the associative method and that shifts of style, tone, and generic expectation are going to be common.

As the next chapter opens the traveler's awareness is turned toward another aspect of the American scene—not mountainous heights and depths now but little towns silent at midnight that exhibit their loneliness briefly before they are swallowed up into the flow of darkness past the windows. Inside the train the boy listens to the conversation in the smoking car, which turns on two American subjects appropriate to autumn—baseball and elections. This is good talk now among the group of Altamont citizens, leisurely talk, of the sort that can set a scene and convey predominant attitudes in the opening scene of a play, before the major characters and their problems begin to emerge. In their drawling, joking way the men reveal their secret distaste for Woodrow Wilson and their reluctant support for Cox. There is a brutal quality of grab in their exchanges that runs counter to the generous American landscape. Mr. Flood, for example, sums it up in Babbitt's idiom:

> "We're tired of hearin' bunk that doesn't pay and we want to hear some bunk that does—an' we're going to vote for the crook that gives it to us. . . . Do you know what we all want—what we're lookin' for? . . . We want a piece of the breast with lots of gravy—an' the boy that promises us the most is the one we're for! . . . Cox! Hell! All of you know Cox has no more chance of getting in than a snowball in hell." (p. 41)

But when the question is put to Mr. Flood about whom he will vote for, the reply is "Who? Me? . . . Why, hell, you ought to know that without asking. Me—I'm a Democrat, ain't I?—don't I publish a Democratic newspaper? I'm going to vote for Cox. of course."

The men now turn to Eugene and question him about his family, and in this way Wolfe makes use of extensive expository dialogue to bring in characterizations of Mr. Gant, Luke Gant, and the dead brother Ben. But in the midst of the talk in which Eugene shyly, reluctantly answers questions, we have two interruptions, memories of his father and of Ben, that reveal the depth of feeling which Eugene cannot openly express. The images of the father are heroic in their vigor: Gant with his "earth-devouring stride" bringing meat home to the family; and the images are historic in their associations: Gant as a boy near the battlefield of Gettysburg, Gant awaiting his brother's return from the battle. In these visions Gant and Eugene are surrounded by the presence of America, and the past and present merge: "And the great stars of America blaze over them, the vast and lonely earth broods around them, then as now, with its secret and mysterious presences, and then as now, the million-noted ululation of the night throngs up from silence the song of all its savage, dark, and measureless fecundity" (p. 58).

The memory of Ben is different in form. It is a dramatic vignette: Eugene, aged twelve, visiting his brother at the newspaper office, is given a surprise birthday present, a gold watch and chain engraved with his name and the date. When Ben asks him if he knows what a watch is for, Eugene in his inarticulate gratitude replies, "To keep time with." As the scene in memory ends the choral voice moves forward intoning: "To keep time with! What is this dream of time, this strange and bitter miracle of living?" Gradually the chant becomes an elegy for Ben: "For now October has come back again, the strange and lonely month comes back again, and you will not return. Up on the mountain, down in the valley, deep, deep in the hill, Ben—cold, cold, cold" (p. 53).

The remainder of the train journey is taken up with some remarkable linguistic play that develops out of the situation of Eugene and two other young fellows getting drunk. I am inclined to call it montage because of the cinematographic quality of the spectacle and because it is made up of condensed, abruptly changing images and fragments of talk. The beginning of it assuredly has the film camera's cosmic vantage as it pans in toward the scene: "So here they are now, three atoms on the huge breast of the indifferent earth, three youths out of a little town walled far away within the great rim of the silent mountains, already a distant, lonely dot upon the immense and sleeping visage of the continent." As the sequence develops a number of elements are merged and, in particular, American motifs are inserted. We have the clickety-clack of the train, the drunken voices of the boys, the moonlight blazing down over Virginia, the voices of passengers at small towns bidding goodbye as they board the train, and the personifications of Death and Pity riding their horses to the beat of a Virgilian line: "Quadrupedante putrem sonitu quatit ungula campum." The drunken babble plays with language: with Elizabethan English, with the moonlight ("beaming, gleaming, seeming" and so on) in Virginia, with the Latin hoofbeats ("campum . . . campum . . . quadrupedante . . . putrem . . . putrem . . . putrem" and so on), and at one point a voice even imitates Mark Twain's raftsmen in a wild boast "I'm a bellybusting bastard from the state of old Catawba—a rootin' tootin' shootin' son of a bitch from Saw Tooth Gap in Buncombe," etc. The exuberance over the train journey leads into wishes to run the train into the west, the plains of Kansas or the fertile earth of Minnesota. Meanwhile counterpointing with silence, the moon is bathing a cinematographically viewed American continent—seacoast, mountain, desert, river, woodland—and sleep lies across the faces of the nation (pp. 68-76).

Only two more units remain in the opening section. The first is a five-paragraph chapter which describes daybreak and the steady progress of the train in the quiet of morning—an obvious allaying of the wild disorder of the previous chapter. The second brings Eugene to Baltimore to visit his father in the hospital—a unit made up of contrasting pictures of Gant—the man's youth and again the boyhood memory of the Confederate soldiers marching to Gettysburg, including his future wife's Uncle Bacchus; over against this, the withered, sick old man unable to communicate with his sons. Eugene leaves, knowing he will never see his father again, as the wandering motif is picked up by the whistle of the train: "Then he turned swiftly and went to meet it—and all the new lands, morning, and the shining city" (p. 86).

It is a remarkable mixture. *Of Time and the River* has done all the things a novel should do at its outset: it has introduced the principal characters whose presences (including the dead brother) are going to be important now and again in the book, and it has made clear the initial situation of the boy's escaping to the North. It has developed thematic motifs of wandering and home, the yearning for a father, the furious hunger of youth, and the puzzlement over time and mortality. At the same time the American geographical sweep, the regional contrasts, the place names, the politics and games have been worked into the scene, the talk, and the narrator's rhythmic assertions. The generic mixture is even more remarkable: novel, essay, choral ode, descriptive travelogue, oratorical discourse, dramatic vignette, cinematographic montage. The whole book continues this way for its 900 pages, whether the scene be Boston, New York City, the Hudson River Valley, Old Catawba, England, or France.

What we have been led to see is that Wolfe has no large-scale narrative gift. He does not write novels in the way that recent critical theorizing has begun to restrict that term. But he has extraordinary literary talents that are expressed in fiction, and what I have been moving toward is a simple generic theory of fiction that will accommodate Wolfe's work and associate it with other works of its kind.

The first distinction to make is between novelistic fiction and lyric fiction (and by fiction I mean an imaginative representation of life which is "made-up" and in which the characters live by the special laws of that fictive world). The distinction is not based on characterization as in Frye's theory but rather on structure. Novelistic fiction develops by means of probability: one event causes the next to happen, which brings about the next, and so on. Lyric fiction develops by means of association: this is related to this, which is related to this, and so on.

But longer works of lyric fiction need to borrow from novelistic fiction some additional organizational schemes in order to contain the associations, otherwise the order of art would dissolve into the disorder of human mental activity. The simplest scheme of organization that it takes over is based on time, and segments of autobiography and biography are commonly used. The result is either the *Bildungsroman* or something that used to be called the novel of character but is not really a novel—a work like MacKenzie's *The Man of Feeling*. A second organizational scheme is based on time and space: the journey. Familiar examples of this device in lyric fiction are the romantic wanderings of a hero in search of life —as in Goethe's *Wilhelm Meister*—or the adventures of the picaro when they are aimless—as in Melville's *Omoo*. Schemes based on space alone are not common in either kind of fiction because the reader absorbs the work in time, and it is difficult for him to adapt himself to an arrangement that implies: this happened at the time this was happening, while at the same time this was happening, and so on. But one finds occasional experiments in short sections of long works: the market scene in *Madame*

Bovary, the wandering rocks episode in *Ulysses*, the party in *Point Counterpoint*. In fact, counterpoint has come to be the term usually applied to these spatial arrangements. If the material is brought together from parts of already existing units, I suggest the term collage. Dos Passos "Newsreels" come first to mind as an example.

But if the principle of organization in a work of lyric fiction is an association of thoughts—which is to say: this thought suggests this, which jumps to this, and so on —then the stream-of-consciousness product results. The work may be a long sequence arising in a single mind like Dorothy Richardson's eight-volume work *Pilgrimage*, or it may present the thoughts of several minds like Faulkner's *The Sound and the Fury*. Additional strengthening of thought relationships may be introduced, such as thematic associations or more oblique governing schemes like myth. If the presentation of ideas is dialectic, then we are likely to have Utopian fictions, such as Bellamy's *Looking Backward* or B. F. Skinner's *Walden II*.

But these additional organizing schemes are more likely to be found in parts of fictional works or mixed together in the work as a whole. Thus a work may employ autobiography, myth, stream of consciousness passages, counterpointed materials, and so on—as does *Look Homeward, Angel*. At times even novelistic fiction may employ lyric sections, such as the interchapters of Steinbeck's *The Grapes of Wrath* or the time-machine device of Mailer's *The Naked and the Dead*. The effect of these generic mixtures is to increase the scope of the work.[20]

Lyric fiction, using the whimsical habits of human thought-progression, strains at any bounds. Thus it is

20. William Empson in his discussion of *Henry IV, Part I* in *Some Versions of the Pastoral* (London, 1935) makes this point very well. See also Leonard Lutwack, "Mixed and Uniform Prose Styles in the Novel," *Journal of Aesthetics and Art Criticism*, XVIII (1960), 350-357, where the critic argues that stylistic mixture creates an illusion of increased complexity in a fictional world.

likely to wander away from fiction into other genre, or to absorb other genre into itself. As we implied earlier, the personal essay is a parallel form to lyric fiction—both use the associative method of development, although one addresses the reader directly whereas the other brings him into a fictional world. Because of this, lyric fiction is likely to drop from time to time into personal essay, as Wolfe's works do, or to push on the one side toward lyric poetry (as in Huxley's *Ape and Essence*) or on another side toward oratorical address (as in Dos Passos' peroration in *The Big Money*, "all right, we are two nations.")

We have seen all these manifestations in Wolfe's *Of Time and the River*, but we still need a term that would apply to a work of lyric fiction which displays complex organizational and stylistic variety, including the characteristic features of other genres. Earlier I used the term thematic anthology for "No Door," but this term implies both too much restriction (thematic) and too much looseness (anthology). At one time I likened *Of Time and the River* to the epic in many of its characteristics, but since the term epic is so generically opposed to the term lyric, we cannot make use of it. In my own searching about I have considered such terms as chrestomathy or miscellany but rejected them because of their connotations. I looked over German terms and seriously considered *Heldenleben*, but then put it aside. Finally I struck on the term thesaurus, which carries meanings of treasury, store house, repository, besides having associations with learning and with verbal abundance, and I decided to use it as the basis for a new literary term—fictional thesaurus. A fictional thesaurus is a long literary work made up of short units in prose or verse in which the parts are joined together by association of ideas rather than by probable and necessary development. It displays a mixture of styles and variations in mood but, taken together, presents a coherent thematic statement or view of life. It achieves unity by its association with the actions of a single character or a closely-related group of characters and sometimes by the voice of a single narrator or spokesman. It may rise to epic dignity by an elevation of style and by a heroic stylization of character along with a thematic reflection of cultural or national customs, values, and beliefs.

Thus Wolfe's *Of Time and the River* can be placed in the same company with other works that have always caused generic difficulty, such as Waldo Frank's *City Block*, Joyce's *Ulysses*, Dos Passos' *U.S.A.*, Cummings' *Eimi*, Huxley's *Ape and Essence,* and Jean Toomer's *Cane.* Fictional thesaurus as a literary category is bounded on its sides by other works which strain at generic limitation. As fictional thesaurus extends toward narrative, it blends into large-scale novelistic works that have a few stylistic variations like *The Grapes of Wrath*. As it leans toward pure lyric, it merges into works like Whitman's *Song of Myself* or Norman O. Brown's *Love's Body*.

To make generic identification of a single work or a body of work is not to evaluate it. To be sure, scope and variety are literary virtues, but the critic should make other demands having to do with order, and thus he must consider coherence, proportion, density, appropriateness of part to part and part to whole when he approaches a fictional thesaurus. But the important consideration is to acknowledge that these demands will be met in different ways than novelistic fiction meets them. For instance, the very fact of generic mixture tends to place emphasis on part rather than whole, and this feature lends an anthology-like quality to most of the works I have just referred to and, in fact, it leads to the habit readers have of revisiting the works later for the reading of chosen parts. Critical discussion must take into account, then, that certain literary peculiarities will arise out of the genre itself.

We stopped our discussion of Wolfe's development as

a literary artist with *Of Time and the River*. If we had traced it further, we would have observed the same procedure, the same experimenting, the same floundering until he had compiled another fictional thesaurus, *The Web and the Rock*, the huge work that Edward Aswell published in three separate volumes after Wolfe's death.

This last period had its gains and its losses. One of its losses is a serious one for American literature. No Wolfe scholar has ever looked at the Publisher's Note in *Of Time and the River* without a sigh of regret, for it promised four more volumes of the Eugene Gant thesaurus. Two of them, "The October Fair" and "The Hills Beyond Pentland," were announced as already written. When Wolfe decided to abandon his mammoth project, he left unfinished a great American work of heroic scale. We can see plainly that parts of it went into *The Web and the Rock* but we cannot grant that these altered parts are completely congruent with the first two volumes. If he had gone on to complete the projected series, some of the questions of genre that have troubled his literary position would have been resolved. As it is, we now have two incomplete heroic sequences. Bad editorial advice and a poor critical climate caused him to drop one; early death cut him off from work on the other. We as critics and readers can deal with this incompleteness best by being aware of Wolfe's procedures and by seeing the unfinished masterworks in a new generic perspective.

The Discussion

MR. PAYNE   I have listened to the presentation of Wolfe almost as *sui generis,* and I am struck by the accuracy of the description, but at the same time puzzled, and a little bothered, by the implication that from now on when we look at Wolfe, we must work with him in terms of a definition that is peculiar to him. It strikes me that we still must come to terms with him within the broader concept of the novel. Granted he was a particular kind of novelist, that he did not work in the Henry James vein of the novel, still he would write fiction, large chunks of prose fiction that must be so evaluated, and I wonder what your definition does in terms of this.

MR. KENNEDY   As I see it, the problem of literary theorizing, and particularly in connection with questions of genre, is merely to get a terminology forward so discussion can prevail. As a matter of fact, I am a person who tends to be a little more reluctant than most to make literary evaluations. I generally regard some of the principal functions of criticism as having as their purpose to identify, to describe, to classify—things of that sort. Because of this, over the years I have come to see so many narrow approaches to literary work that I distrust them. Narrow evaluators come to some snap judgment on the work which does not do justice to the work as a whole. I may be, because of my long association with the Wolfe material, a little bit more this way than most people; but when I discuss works in my modern American fiction course I purposely bring in novels, works of fiction, that are generically troublesome. I sum up very early in the course the Frye genre material in order to get the terminology before the students—there isn't much more that one does with it except keep the student from reading a book like Nabokov's *Pale Fire* and saying to himself, This is nonsense. What one does in reading a work like that, or John Barth's *The Floating Opera,* is to see that this is a work that is in a different kind of category, and therefore we have to judge it in different ways.

What I was trying to do with this paper was to place Wolfe in a kind of special category because he has to go into one. What I was doing was setting up a kind of theory of fiction of my own—Frye takes characterization as his basis for setting up those four forms. I took structure because empirically it seemed to be a way that I could get hold of the problem. I am very much aware now —much more aware than I was before—of this distinction between Wolfe's kind of fictional work and those like Edith Wharton's *The Age of Innocence,* where you have a situation and it grows and it affects a character in a certain way, and the character changes, and then a problem develops and then there is interaction, and finally the problem is resolved, and you have the principle of probability operating there. Since Wolfe does not use this principle, I thought it was important to try to see in what way he can be seen to develop. Because otherwise what do we do with *Of Time and the River*, which is the document that I particularly wanted to work with?

We see that the work starts in a certain way and all of a sudden veers in such a way that you have to account for it within its own terms or else say, "Well, this piece of work is only a jumble." This is what I was trying to do. After all, with literary terminology, one sets up the working definitions that one wishes just in order to have terminology so discussion can go forward. As Sweeney says in *Sweeney Agonistes*, "I've gotta use words when I talk to you." And this is a way that I hoped to talk in a subtly different fashion about Wolfe's fiction. When you say "Well, they are novels," you are going back to another set of terminology. I could talk to you in those terms about it, but not nearly so well as in the terms that I was trying to set up, particularly with this distinction between novelistic fiction and lyric fiction.

This is the reason why reviewers had such a terrible time with Joyce's *Ulysses* when it first came out. We can deal with it now; we are used to the works that are put together in these unusual ways. And it was the same thing with some of the disjunctive poetry that emerged. If you would read Louis Untermeyer's first comment on "The Love Song of J. Alfred Prufrock" as compared to what he has in his anthology now, you would think he was a fool. It is just that in 1917 he had certain generic expectations and they were not fulfilled, so he said, "Throw it out, it is no good."

MR. HUTTON You talked very interestingly throughout the paper about the idea of the voice in Wolfe, and as far as I could gather there were three types of voices: journalistic, autobiographical, and the voice of the personal essay; and then you began to bring these all together into what you called the communal voice. I don't quite understand the definition of Wolfe's communal voice, or what you would call the communal voice.

MR. KENNEDY This is a problem that I began to notice in dealing with twentieth-century fiction in connection with other works. Have you ever noticed when you are reading Faulkner that you are going along in a certain way and suddenly from somewhere else comes some other kind of voice than the one that you have been listening to?—call it whatever name you want, mythic voice or earth voice, or whatever. Faulkner tries to tip you off to it in a work like "The Bear," for instance, in the fourth section, by having all the odd syntactical arrangements—no capital letters and things of that sort. It seems to me that one has to become aware when a shift in voice takes place. We have an omniscient narrator who talks in a certain way, and suddenly there is another kind of style and tone. It is almost as if we have someone different talking.

Now, in connection with Wolfe in particular, I was made very much aware of this one time when talking about *The Web and the Rock* with a group of my graduate students. A very perceptive young lady said, "What about this business where the boy is lying in the grass in front of the house, his mother is calling him, and he says something like 'You want me to run a little errand; that is no task for a man. Give me a real task. Is this the kind of thing that Falstaff was asked to do? Is this the kind of thing that you would call upon Hercules to do, or Kubla Khan?' " The student asked who was talking here. It is not that twelve-year-old boy's voice (though it reflects the boy's attitude toward his mother), but it is the rhetoric of platform oratory. Well, this is the narrator, yes, but projecting himself so that he speaks for the boy in this way. Why?

In putting this paper together, I tried to look at each work that I was dealing with to see what was happening as far as narrators were concerned. I noticed in particular when Wolfe shifted material and took pieces of work that were written in the first person that he had published in periodicals in 1932 and transferred them to *Of Time and the River*. What he did at these times was to make slight alterations in them as to where the voice came from. Now, if a first-person narrator is saying, "I remember this, and I remember that, and I felt this, and I felt that," he cannot suddenly say, "October has come again, has come again," and go into one of those long discourses that is not appropriate to the "I" who is speaking, so Wolfe makes that second voice come from somewhere else. A voice in the wind comes to Eugene when he is up there in Cambridge and he hears the voice calling, or the ancestral voices come to him when he is going to the city on the train. Or he in some way associates the voice with an old man or with age. Well, as soon as Wolfe changes to a third-person narrator for *Of Time and the River*, he does not have to do that any more; he can thrust these things right in. The reason he can do this is that we as readers over the years have heard someone like the omniscient narrator in Dickens address so many oratorical things to us, or the narrator in somebody like Hardy's novels address so many direct and profound statements to us, that when the author is ready to make this shift, he makes it and does not worry about it. The result is that at times the narrator describes action, links together material, offers descriptions; there are times when this moves him to a more turgid kind of descriptive style. Then there are some other times when it seems to me that there is a voice that is a communal voice, one that is no longer just the narrator describing things to help the reader out and bringing to him some kind of material that ought to be conveyed for the reader's information; but the narrator is now acting as a kind of national spokesman or some kind of universal voice of wisdom. This is a distinctive feature of Wolfe's narrator.

MR. HUTTON The only point that I would like to mention again is that it seems to me your presentation is more than a man uniquely American voicing something uniquely American; it seems to be more classic, like the choral arrangement of people saying things that are beyond the characters themselves.

MR. KENNEDY The style is one of the things that helps us to see this. If you analyze one of those passages closely, you will see the way the materials are presented, particularly the way questions are asked (the way questions are not answered, too, is another aspect of it), and then go to one of those Sophoclean choruses, in *Antigone,* for example, you will see that this is the kind of thing that Wolfe was doing. He didn't have as good a translation as Robert Fitzgerald for a model; he only had Gilbert Murray, but he did pretty well.

MR. HOLMAN In shifting from first person to third person, particularly with regard to these voices, didn't Wolfe achieve perhaps license instead of freedom? In the first person presentation he had to have some kind of control to justify the presence of this material in some dramatic sense. When he moves to the third person he must depend on the reader to recognize changes in tone and rhetoric in order to define these things that I think most of us feel that he wasn't always successful in communicating. There is a certain kind of shift in time perspective as well as in voice that begins to occur in this method that the use of a first-person narration, if it had been maintained, would have prevented. Do you feel this?

MR. KENNEDY I would have to respond in two ways. In the first place, I agree with you that various kinds of devices that can hold him down, hold his materials together, strengthen whatever results. On the other hand, you recognize when you perceive a shift to another kind of voice that you've got a different kind of book.

MR. HOLMAN So the question that I now ask is: Which kind of book did he intend to write when he actually wrote *Of Time and the River*? He wrote a great deal of the material that actually went into it in first-person narrative.

MR. KENNEDY I don't think that the way that some of those materials are finally put into that book or into *The Web and the Rock,* the second part especially, are quite as well suited as they might be—in particular with respect to the linking between one part and another. Usually where there is a large white space on the page it means that Wolfe has taken something out of the bottom of his manuscript box and said, "I think this will go in here." What is interesting is the fact that since he created this kind of special perspective on his own world in his own life and since he lived in it so intensely during those creative periods, he was able to select, I think, extraordinarily well. It is often surprising in examining manuscripts to see where something else was before, when you thought it fitted so beautifully in this particular place. There are the successes as well as the failures.

MISS GREEN I would like to ask a similar question concerning the success of these two voices. You seem to imply that there is a tangent set up between the narrative voice (if one can call it that) and the communal voice. If you feel that this creates an incongruity in texture, do you think that he manages to unify the voices successfully?

MR. KENNEDY One of the things that you are implying is that you have this special kind of generic expectation; the shift should not take place, you say to yourself. I want to go for a moment now to that little sequence where in Eugene's memory there is the birthday present that Ben gives him—the watch. And what's it for? It's to keep time with. And you get a white space in the text [*Of Time and the River*, p. 52]. Then we get this communal voice with its ode on time. Now it seems to me that this is a very appropriate kind of theme for the communal voice to develop, and to pick up the very phrase "To keep time with" is, of course, a fine link with that material. Something else that seems to take place, however, is the fact that we've got a scene in a smoking car, the dialogue, the language that is being exchanged here is very ordinary and coarse and down-to-earth. When the memory of the brother Ben comes in, the shift in voice gives a special opportunity for this heightened language to convey that feeling which Eugene has about his brother Ben.

The reason I relate it to the drama is that when I was a college student I put together for the Campus Theater at UCLA a series of things that I had taken out of Wolfe's works, and I don't remember what I called it—"An Evening with Thomas Wolfe," or "Aspects of the American Scene," or "Aspects of Wolfe's America," or something like that. I selected certain scenes. I can remember, for instance, there was the scene of Eugene discussing who was the greatest prose writer in the world with Eddy Murphy; there was the scene of Martha Upshaw and the confrontation with her dying husband when Eugene was present; there was the scene between the old people in the Hotel Albert when they talk about what they had for dinner; there was a scene with people viewing death— one of those from "Death the Proud Brother"—and the ambulance people are there, and some Greenwich Village sophisticates come by, and there are various responses to this death scene; there was a little episode with George Webber and one of the so-called lion hunters; there was the scene where Mrs. Pierce asks Eugene Gant what he does when he goes out and walks around at night. I don't remember what all of them were, but there were quite a few and they were arranged in such a way that the narrator was present too, and like the stage manager in *Our Town* he comments on the action that is going on before him. It was extremely effective to have this scene which was enacted between the character Eugene and his brother when the watch was given as a present; then to have the narrator to come in and make his commentary.

Now that was an example where you just have a chunk here, followed by another chunk there. It's more interesting sometimes when it is counterpointed, as that scene with Mrs. Pierce about Eugene walking around the city at night. She says to him, "What do you do on these prowling expeditions?" He is inarticulate about it, and then going through his mind presumably (and the narrator comments for him) are all the magnificent and varied scenes of the city. And when she says, "My dear boy, what on earth do you ever find in a place like that to interest you?" he merely says, "People." But the narrator produces the great catalogue of the people of the city. Then to her question "The Bridge? What bridge?" the narrator gives the discourse on the Brooklyn Bridge. We have a very effective scene here that can be staged, and it works dramatically the way that I have seen it. I imagined it this way as a reader even before I picked it out and tried to stage it. This is one of the ways I would try— more than just by presenting something to you as an answer—I would try to demonstrate the answer by going off in another entirely different generic approach to it.

MISS GREEN You have implied, then, that it is the thematic stimulus that serves as your associative principle between the voices. Is this true?

MR. KENNEDY Yes.

MISS GREEN Well, that is the associative principle at work here, too.

MR. SINGH One comes to have the suspicion that between the detractors of Wolfe on one side, because of the charges of formlessness against him, and his admirers on the other, who have tried to justify his lack of form, there exists the same sort of relationship that exists between segregationists and black power militants. I think that most people would agree that there is a lack of form, but I think in this close circle we are at a loss to know what it is that holds these narratives together; and I think that before evaluating the technique it is necessary to define the metaphysics, and often Wolfe's technique bears a very close relationship to his themes and what he was trying to say. Now I will not go into a long description of what I think is the best example of this but I will sum it up in a sentence, as I view it, and that is "the lonely and mortal individual's quest for a meaningful relationship with an infinite and timeless universe" and that is why we find these seemingly puzzling definitions of references to man's isolation, transience, and quest for certitude. I found these extremely baffling in the beginning until I thought maybe what he was trying to see is how does the little small humble mortal individual fit into the frighteningly vast universe and this infinite time, and because of this theme I think the movement of his novels does look like a stream that flows into a larger stream and that becomes a vast river that goes into the ocean. And then you see this in the first novel, the birth into the family, and then in the next he leaves the old southern town and goes out into the world of the North; in the next novel he leaves his self-absorption, and he involves himself into the life of another person, Esther, and then again it ends with his disillusionment; and finally in the last of his novels, death itself means release into lands larger than life. Now another aspect in which I think Wolfe's metaphysics is reflected in his techniques—by this time he has gotten over the self-absorption and intense confinement to his own self and begins to work with the larger life of humanity, and similarly his characters—one very peculiar thing about most of his characters almost the first time you meet them; he tells you what is going to happen to them.

MR. KENNEDY This is an extensive and comprehensive commentary on Wolfe's work reaching from its very beginning to its end. There are so many places that I would like to pick it up. Actually you and I approach the works very differently. I tend to start with technique, and you start with the world that you find within the work. Where can we meet in answering a question or two back and forth? Let me pick up two things that I would like to say in connection with your commentary. One, you were saying something to the effect that Wolfe's central character has a certain kind of relationship to the world in which he lives and that he moves in a certain way and his world changes, and then he has the love relationship; there is disillusionment, and things come to an end, and so forth. In some ways this problem of the changing worlds exists.

I spoke of the fact that he left two incomplete mammoth works—just take the first one for a moment. It seems to me, from what little I can get hold of in seeing where I think you would go, that I should point out that Wolfe planned some kind of movement toward a resolution of these problems. For one thing, he had the intention to have Eugene's father-figure discovered in his editor, and he also planned to have Eugene discover the artist's control of his material, and I think that both of these resolutions were going to emerge in that book that Wolfe tentatively entitled "The Death of the Enemy." The coming to such a resolution would have possibly changed the way that a critic who starts out with the world view tends to look at the work as a whole.

Another thing which must be added is the fact that one of the great problems of Wolfe criticism is that we have these published works in our hands; and we have the implication, particularly by his second editor, Edward Aswell, that they represent the kind of stylistic progression that he described in his "Note on Thomas Wolfe." But this is not entirely true. Some of the extraordinarily comprehensive rhetorical flights came from very late periods of Wolfe's writing. Some of the most nostalgic and intense gatherings together of the memories of his boyhood come very late. I am referring, for example, to the chapter called "Three O'Clock" which is one of the finest pieces in *The Web and the Rock*. This is very late, but it is combined with earlier materials. So it is very hard to make these comments about stylistic shifts and changes. Now it is true that Wolfe makes a late excursion into satirical material where the style is somewhat different, and a little more plain style. This probably develops out of his dictating material and then having some of it cut down somewhat by his faithful editor. Some materials that he dictated in a very automatic way, possibly when he was very tired, have a plainer quality about them than some of the other material; and so it is hard to tell about the direction of Wolfe's style.

I, in my work with Wolfe, have tried as much as I possibly could to hold to specific units that I knew he created himself and then make certain speculations, and likewise I have tried to see the material in the order in which he composed it, rather than in the order in which it was published, and to make sure that I was aware of earlier or later materials. It is a very interesting and perplexing problem. There are times when I feel like one of the higher critics of the Bible. When you get someone like Maxwell Perkins and Edward Aswell they are like rabbinical councils or priestly scribes that come in and make changes later, and a critic has to try to figure out what the essential document was before the meddlers began to tamper with it. One has also a sense of time—I do at any rate—in connection with these comments about the communal voice. There are times when we have Wolfe attempting to speak not just for himself but to speak for a national concept of some sort; and I think this does something to his work—if he conceives that he has a mission. Thank you for your illuminating comment.

MR. SINGH Just one other point. You can trust the passages in which he describes his life at Chapel Hill—and similar scenes from Europe and life in New York. I particularly recall his description of himself and his first day at UNC at Chapel Hill, in the first novel and in the third novel. In the first one, *Look Homeward, Angel,* he describes himself as some sort of latter-day Sophocles, poet and genius, and going to enlighten the world. In the second one, he has got himself as a clumsy, gawky freshman unsure of himself. Apparently this transition goes from looking at himself from within to the second description indicating that the narrator is without. There are a number of these passages which clearly show in the later compositions a matter of change of perspective.

MR. KENNEDY   Yes, indeed.

MR. DRAKE   You touched on something just at the end of your preceding remarks that has always disturbed me about Wolfe—the question of speaking for the nation. I have always suspected that Wolfe was the spiritual son of Walt Whitman, and I find Whitman extremely unpersuasive in poems like "Song of Myself" when he tries quite literally to eat up the whole North American continent. He is much more persuasive when he has got something to hold him down that he knows, like "Crossing Brooklyn Ferry" and "Out of the Cradle Endlessly Rocking," which is not to say that I think Wolfe is most persuasive when he is most autobiographical.

MR. KENNEDY   I am interested in your comment. May I ask you a question: Who is a poet that you have particular admiration for?

MR. DRAKE   I enjoy factitious oversimplication. I like to tell students that all modern American poetry descends in two major streams: one from Walt Whitman and one from Emily Dickinson.

MR. KENNEDY   A person who has the generic expectations that are associated with the metaphysical poetry that Emily Dickinson writes comes to Walt Whitman and says, "What a mess!"

MR. DRAKE   One of the most profound and pertinent critical comments I have ever read on the art of fiction is something that E. M. Forster just throws out in passing in *Aspects of the Novel.* He is speaking of Miss Bates in Jane Austen's *Emma,* and he says, "We know Miss Bates is a bore, but she doesn't bore us." And I think volumes could not say more than that.

MR. KENNEDY   To get at such a situation one should know what the techniques are which make that come to be. As you can see, it was my intention tonight to try to work with techniques to see what it is that we have got, and what kinds of classifications we can make when we examine the material.

Richard Walser

The Angel and the Ghost

As is well known, Thomas Wolfe's working title for *Look Homeward, Angel* was "O Lost." After Scribners had accepted the manuscript for publication, Wolfe was asked to choose another title, since "O Lost" had hardly the attractive ring to lure purchasers of a first novel. Apparently Wolfe was not annoyed by the request; in any case, he went to work jotting down possibilities in his notebook. It was a routine he followed thereafter, and fortunate he was in the titles of his books. He managed to make all of them poetic yet easy to remember—not an easy trick by any means. Richard S. Kennedy tells how he cast aside such uninviting and melancholy echoes from his manuscript as "Alone Alone" and "Prison of Earth" and "The Lost Language," and then hit upon the words from "Lycidas."[1]

Look Homeward, Angel was a happy choice, but it must be remembered that this change in title, coming long after the manuscript had been virtually completed, caused a shift away from what had been the dominant symbol. Now, except to the few cognoscenti, the angel was accepted as the major symbolic figure, and not the haunting, lost ghost heralded in the proem written two years ear-

1. *The Window of Memory: The Literary Career of Thomas Wolfe* (Chapel Hill, 1962), p. 177.

lier.[2] That Wolfe was aware of the confusion the Miltonic title might cause is evinced by his setting down a reminder to himself in his notebook: "Put into final scene of book 'Look Homeward, Angel, now, and melt with ruth.' "[3] But no such full-line reference, or paraphrase of it, appeared in the printed version. Perhaps he decided he did not need to insert the line, for was not the novel already amply supplied with several varied angels to whom the reader might relate the title?

But despite the numerous angels, it has always been difficult to explain the title satisfactorily, to make the angel doubly meaningful within both Milton and Wolfe contexts. Two examples of the troublesome situation will suffice. In 1950 W. P. Albrecht provided an elaborate and ingenious gloss in which Ben is the angel of the "guarded Mount" and Eugene is Lycidas.[4] The lost ghost of the proem is opposed on the next page by the titular angel, who is not lost but secure in eternity. (I must admit that this arrangement seems to me more the result of a book designer's decision than of artistic intention.) In the last chapter Ben insists he is not a ghost, and since the stone angels move about in Ben's presence, the reader is willing to believe that he too is an angel, temporarily making Eugene the ghost. So far, so good. "As the angels melt from their stone rigidity," writes Mr. Albrecht, "so does the angel Ben 'melt with ruth,' and the 'hapless' Eugene is wafted 'homeward.' " Lycidas is then "mounted high," and in the same way the lost Eugene is found. "In this sense," the explanation concludes, "Lycidas-Eugene is at least on his way to becoming an 'angel,' and the title is appropriately addressed to Eugene as well as to Ben."

Now, if my condensation is unjust to Albrecht, perhaps

2. Ibid., p. 157.

3. Ibid., p. 177.

4. "The Titles of *Look Homeward, Angel: A Story of the Buried Life,*" *Modern Language Quarterly,* XI (1950), 57.

one reason is that I do not always understand him, that I miss some of the things I want and need to know, such as the identity of the proem ghost, and I fear he has proceeded a posteriori. After all, we remember that the first draft of the manuscript was completed before the title from "Lycidas" was seriously considered.

The second example is much briefer and much, much less rewarding. In this case the commentator quotes the appropriate passage from "Lycidas," then remarks that Milton in his poem "invokes the protector angel St. Michael to turn from foreign threats to weep for a disaster at home. The same meaning may be applied to Wolfe's novel," this critic continues. "Heaven is urged to look toward home and 'melt with ruth' rather than gaze afar for tragic possibilities. Altamont and the Gant family have their own pathetic lives." Questions arise immediately. Is St. Michael the protector of Altamont as well as of England? What is the "disaster at home"? And so on. Here we have a blunt rationalization, with the novel's being forced into fitting a Miltonic pattern without Wolfean textual evidence to support it. I regret to admit that I wrote these sentences myself eight years ago.[5]

For the moment let us leave aside the confusing problem of the title itself and, assuming that the ghost and the angel are the two major figures in the novel, systematically search through it for interpretations of them.

In the printed version of the novel, the word *ghost*, including its inflectional forms and derivatives (e.g., *ghostliness, ghost-kiss*), is, by a careful but not a computerized count, used eighty-six times. For *angel*, the count is forty-seven.[6] If *spirit, haunt, spectre,* and *phan-*

---

5. Richard Walser, *Thomas Wolfe: An Introduction and Interpretation* (New York, 1961), p. 65.

6. The count was made by students in two senior English seminars at North Carolina State University. During our study of *Look Homeward, Angel*, these students also provided illuminating critiques, some of which doubtless have found their way into my paper.

tom—words often synonymous with *ghost*, but rarely
with *angel*—are added, the imbalance in favor of the
ghost over the angel is even more marked. Despite the
prevalence of the ghost image in the book,[7] early critics
by-passed a discussion of it in order to remark on other
aspects which interested them: its sensuous prose, its
narrative vigor, and so on. Generally *Look Homeward,
Angel* was loosely defined as a family chronicle strong in
characterization, overcharged with heady poetry. Presumably the ghost and the angel were part of the heady
poetry. But since 1945, with the publication of Monroe M.
Stearns's article on Wolfe's metaphysics,[8] more attention
has been given the symbology. Stearns proposes con-
vincingly, for instance, that the lost, wind-grieved ghost is
closely linked with the Platonic soul's pre-existence as set
forth in Wordsworth's Intimations Ode. Though Stearns
did not follow up with a detailed analysis of his interpretation, this reading has since been generally accepted.

Kennedy tells how Wolfe settled on the principal symbols when about half the novel had been written, and how
he had been working on it for a year before composing
the opening proem.[9] In the proem Wolfe intones his joy-
less declaration of man's aloneness and his hopeless inability to relate to the world and to the people in it. For
purposes of contrast, he, like Wordsworth, imagines a
prior ideal existence. From it, "naked and alone"[10]

7. In the play *Mannerhouse* (New York, 1948), on which Wolfe
had been working for several years before he began his first novel,
the ghost image is repeatedly used. For instance, Eugene, the hero
of the play, says to his father, "I am living in a world where all the
ghosts are people; all the people ghosts. . . . I must find my way back
to my shades again" (p. 65). See also pp. 74-77, 134, and elsewhere.

8. "The Metaphysics of Thomas Wolfe," *College English*, VI
(1945), 193-199. (This essay is reprinted in Richard Walser, ed., *The
Enigma of Thomas Wolfe: Biographical and Critical Selections*,
Cambridge, Mass., 1953, pp. 195-205.)

9. *The Window of Memory*, pp. 148, 157-158.

10. *Look Homeward, Angel* (New York, 1929), p. 2. Subsequent
page numbers in parentheses are from this edition.

(Wordsworth writes "not in utter nakedness"), man has come into the exile of earth, a stranger and prison-pent (Wordsworth's hyphenation is "prison-house"). Though now lost, man continually seeks to find "the lost lane-end into heaven"—that is, the way back to the radiant state of "God, who is our home" (Wordsworth)—in order once more to see plainly the now "forgotten faces." These faces are the spiritual entities of the mother ("In her dark womb we did not know our mother's face"), the brother ("Which of us has known his brother?"), and the father ("Which of us has looked into his father's heart?"); and they forecast Eliza, Ben, and W. O. Gant, whose exteriors are to be seen on earth but to whom son and brother will remain stranger. The stone, the leaf, the door—all are routes of return, but their entryways cannot be found. Meanwhile man pleads with his ghost of memory ("those shadowy recollections," writes Wordsworth)—a ghost synonymous with an earlier, ideal, intangible self—to come back, to be restored and reinstated. The wind ("The Winds come to me from the fields of sleep" is the way Wordsworth expresses it), unseen but felt, grieves over man but, somewhat like "the devious-cruising Rachel" in the Epilogue of *Moby Dick* searching "after her missing children," cannot find him who is lost (Wordsworth writes, "in darkness lost"). There are other verbal parallels.

The first paragraph of the first chapter of *Look Homeward, Angel* follows this Platonic-Wordsworthian proem and in it, with "the proud coral cry of the cock" (p. 3), the symbolic ghost of the lost ideal paradise is banished, and we are in the very real world where "the soft stone smile of an angel" presides over the harsh lives of a family buffeted about by sorrow and change and, most of all, by Chance.

In the course of the novel, however, never for long are the leitmotifs of the proem to be stilled, though generally the thematic words are echoed in modified form. But on four occasions there is no variation whatsoever in the most memorable of the lines, the crowning hexameter "O lost, and by the wind grieved, ghost, come back again," which, like Spenser's alexandrine, provides a strong emotional heightening to conclude the other lines of the proem. Wolfe places his repetitions in carefully selected spots—spots where he indubitably wishes to emphasize his fundamental theme.

The first repetition comes when the child Eugene looks uncomprehendingly upon the corpse of Grover in St. Louis and "remembered that forgotten face he had not seen in weeks, that strange bright loneliness that would not return" (p. 58). Whether intentional or not, Wolfe's words, a translation of childhood's inarticulate response to an unfamiliar but deeply felt situation, recall Wordsworth's "radiance which was once so bright / . . . now forever taken from my sight." It is then that the "O lost" hexameter is inserted, as though Wolfe were reminding the reader that, as in the case of four-year-old Eugene's sensing the irrecoverable "strange bright loneliness," one's soul best "beholds the light" (Wordsworth) in early childhood.

The second repetition is more than two-hundred pages later in a section of sheer phantasmagoria. At half past three in the morning a drowsy Eugene arises from bed to deliver his newspapers. From the darkness of sleep, symbolic of course of rebirth, Eugene moves realistically but hesitantly and slowly into that other darkness of the earth's night. Called "ghost-eared" and "phantom" (p. 295), he is, half-awake and half-asleep, in a limbo or intermediate state very near indeed to the "hidden land below the rock" (p. 296), so near in fact that it is no longer certain that Eugene is Eugene, and the ghost is the ghost. "Ghost, ghost, who is the ghost?" (p. 295) we read. The speaker here is someone or something to the side of both Eugene and the ghost, or perhaps the speaker is the ghost within Eugene. "Lift up the rock, Eugene, the leaf, the stone, the unfound door. Return, return" (pp. 295-296). The reader feels, his emotions tense, that now, if the opportunity is grasped quickly, it may be possible for Eugene, his identities fused, to return, promptly and immediately, to a place "where darkness . . . is light" (p. 296). The enchanted prose is reminiscent of Wordsworth's lines that, "Though inland far we be, / Our Souls have sight of that immortal sea / Which brought us hither." At this moment, as in similar passages of *Look Homeward, Angel,* there shortly comes the tone of "the grotted coral sea-far horn-note" and a vision of lovely unscaled mer-women "in sea-floor colonnades." Then suddenly those and other sounds and sights are "gone on the wind like bullets," and we hear for the third time "O lost, and by the wind grieved, ghost, come back again."

The chance of possible return is forfeited. Eugene dresses and descends the stairs of Dixieland on the way to his job. Though the occasion for the recovery of lost brightness is past, the mood is still upon him and "the strange ringing in his ears persisted. He listened, like his own ghost, to his footsteps . . . [and] saw, from sea-sunk eyes, the town" (p. 296). As "the music soared," Eugene, no longer a child, cries out: " 'I will remember. When I come to the place, I shall know.' " But Eugene's assurance is not the reader's, for we have been schooled to Wordsworth and we are well aware that, as Eugene grows older, "the lost key opening the prison gates" will be more impossible than ever to find. Thenceforward the wind-grieved ghost will have to make itself manifest in different circumstances, in different people.

Both the third and fourth repetitions come after the idyllic summer scene with Laura on "an island of tender grass" (p. 453) among the wooded hills, at a time when Eugene is deeply in love. In that ecstatic episode, Eugene is as close as he ever will be to an unchanging, a seemingly permanent timelessness. As he clings to Laura, fearful that she may "grow into the tree again" (p. 456)—that is, that she may leave him and be translated into a nonhuman absolute—time is frozen and "the winds are silent." The ghost is entreated to "return not into life, but into magic"—a state, one infers, made possible only by imperishable love, a state "where we have never died." But time does move, the "timeless valley" vanishes, even love is temporary and brief, and we hear the familiar "O lost, and by the wind grieved, ghost, come back again." With the departure of Laura, Eugene is enmeshed once more in everyday life.

In this passage it is not Eugene's ghost of memory reminding him of the preexistent paradise, but the near perfection of love which is equivalent to that lost ideal state. The wind-grieved ghost is hailed not once, but twice. Yet all is useless. Only art will make it possible for Eugene to discover "the lost lane-end into heaven."

Eugene's fear that Laura may "grow into the tree again, or be gone amid the wood like smoke" (p. 456) suggests that the ghost is somehow part of a Wordsworthian pantheism. Though searching for the spiritual ideal, Eugene nevertheless is not, at this time, willing to yield up the physical person of Laura. Half a year later at Christmas, the boy, drunk and very alert and alone at Dixieland, determines to face at last "the Stranger that dwelt in him and regarded him and was him" (p. 494), and in order to do so, he is prepared, in Wolfe's unmistakable idiom, to unwind his life back to his birth and be subtracted into nakedness again. Beyond even prenatal nakedness is a state of existence in which he shall "grow to the earth like a hill or a rock." Eugene waits quietly in the silence of Dixieland for the outset of the rush back through the millennia, but when "no doors were opened," he flees the deserted house.

Even so, the notion of man's identity with nature, his origin in it, is never far from Eugene. The following spring at Easter, he visits Ben in the town where he is working, and there "all the men who had died were making their strange and lovely return in blossom and flower. Ben walked along the streets of the tobacco town looking like asphodel. It was strange to find a ghost there in that place" (p. 507).

These three brief references to the basic pantheistic quality of preexistence have their climax on an October evening later that year. After Ben's funeral, "as the wind howled in the bleak street" (p. 577) and as "Eliza sat before the fire at Dixieland" talking about Ben, a puzzled Eugene suddenly realizes that he is confronted by a "little bright and stricken thing" (obviously his dead brother), telling him, during a remarkable colloquy, that he must escape, must find himself—in short, that the "lost boy" must, Ben insists, "find me" (p. 578). Here it is clear that Ben is the sacrifice necessary to purchase Eugene's emancipation, his escape, his fulfillment. In an effort to comply with the command, to understand what Ben would have of him, Eugene goes to the cemetery and stands beside the new grave of his brother. He meditates on change and certain irredeemable loss, then slowly perceives, with an emerging philosophic maturity, that not all things pass away. There are, in fine, some things which will come again. "Spring, the cruellest and fairest of the seasons, will come again. And the strange and buried men will come again, in flower and leaf.... And Ben will come again" (pp. 582-583). Then, for the sixth and last time and the fifth repetition, Wolfe sounds his refrain "O lost, and by the wind grieved, ghost, come back again!" (p. 583). At this luminous moment no longer is man's impulse for return a despairing one. Going back to paradise may not be possible for haloed infancy or uncorrupted adolescence or brief love here on earth, but return is most certainly possible "in flower and leaf," in cyclic nature, in un-changing time. Not only can Ben, transmuted, return, but, in Wolfe's last chapter of the novel several dozen pages later, he will indeed do so, though not in flower and leaf.

If the four episodes here recalled are the most sig-nificant ones to analyze when attempting to comprehend Wolfe's dominant symbol, by no means are they his only meaningful references to the ghost. In its role as that part of man which is "lost" in the "prison of this earth," the ghost frequently is called up to lament the rude condi-tions which the fallen gods, the strangers in exile, must endure. Often it is not a prenatal existence, but simply a prior, more happy existence which the ghost remembers. It is with the protagonist Eugene that the ghost is most familiar, but W. O. Gant and Ben also have their private phantoms, and, at least on one occasion, that disagreeable fellow Steve.

For Gant, an aging and doomed man more apt to be recalling his vigorous youth rather than a prior existence, the word is often *spectre*. Following Cynthia's death, thinking he has tuberculosis, W. O. "turned westward," "alone and lost again," a "gaunt spectre" (p. 6), his earlier life becoming "the spectre years." Yet after the first winter in Altamont, some of the lost vigor returns, and his voice takes on "the ghost of the old eagerness" (p. 9). But a second reversal comes upon his meeting Eliza's family. At that point his fate is sealed. He "heard the spectre moan of the wind, he was entombed in loss and dark-ness . . . (and) he saw that he must die a stranger" (p. 15) in a land foreign to him. In his ill health he seems "a "spectre in waxen yellow" (p. 608).

Like W. O.'s ghost, Steve's is a reminder of a better, a more virtuous past. In his early twenties Steve was an un-attractive bully, objectionable on almost every count, but Wolfe writes that there was still to be observed "in his swagger walk, the ghost of his ruined boyishness" (p.

150). Ben's ghost, on the contrary, at least for most of the novel, is a ghost existing in present time, a lonely ghost singing in a "thin humming ghost's voice" (p. 94). As a newspaperboy Ben comes and goes "like a phantom" (p. 112). Years later, at Christmas, he prowls through Dixieland "like a familiar ghost" (p. 491). To Eugene it seems that Ben's spirit-ghost, in a way similar to his angel, is seeking "to find some entrance into life" (pp. 113, 447), the life of ordinary people, so aware is Ben of how quickly he is retreating into stone and leaf.

In a novel as rich in symbols as *Look Homeward, Angel*, these few citations must not lure the reader into forgetting that the angel is the principal device for illuminating the essential characteristics of W. O. Gant and Ben, and that Eugene too has his minor angel. But the ghost, not the angel, is the primary emblem for Eugene from birth on—the source of his power, his understanding, his art. The difficulty is, as we know, that the ghost is lost and must be found, that in fact Eugene is lost and must be found before his innate gifts of potency and creativity can be realized.

Even in his crib, with an adult intelligence presumably derived from prior existence, Eugene senses that he is "lost." While gazing at the huge people who walk about his crib, "he heard a great bell ringing faintly, as if it sounded undersea, and as he listened, the ghost of memory walked through his mind, and for a moment he felt that he had almost recovered what he had lost" (p. 38). Later, at the time he enters the first grade, even Eliza is aware that the boy, "fed by the lost communications of eternity," is "his own ghost, haunter of his own house, lonely to himself and to the world" (p. 81).

That the ghost is more than merely "the ghost of memory" becomes evident in a kaleidoscopic chapter concerning Eugene at the age of eleven. The boy hears "the ghostly ticking of his life" (p. 191). He plucks "out of the ghostly shadows a million gleams of light." Contrasted with "the ghostly shadows"—the darkness, the exile, the noncreative state—the "gleams of light" connote the utopia beyond apparent recapture, the creative act. These "gleams" are, as Wolfe writes, "Fixed in no-time," "frozen in time" (p. 192) and thus are experiences suitable for use in the creation of art. Their "white living brightness" makes "all things else . . . more awful because of them." For instance, among the "gleams of light" seen from a passing train are "a little station by the rails . . . a wisp-haired slattern . . . a cool-lipped lake at dawn" (p. 191). Eugene knows that Chance has provided these experiences, and it is his duty to give them "a pattern, and movement." When these experiences are frozen in time it is then that they are reality—they are the genesis of the creative act—and Eugene's "sense of unreality" (p. 192) comes only when he imagines "the woman, when the train had passed," so to speak, "as walking back into the house, lifting a kettle from the hearth embers. Thus life turned shadow, the living lights went ghost again." As his meditations continue Eugene ponders how experience has no existence except what each man gives to it, no permanence except in the creative act. This brief digression from the straight narrative ends with the fish swimming "upward from the depth" (p. 193)—an indication that the impulse for creativity originates in pre-existent perfection.

A second fantasy set in frozen time absorbs Eugene one winter evening while walking home with Gant from the moving-picture theater. From an idealized fictive trance in which the boy sees himself as a Wild West hero playing the role of the Stranger, the Dixie Ghost, who shoots the gambler dead and wins the girl, he moves to other reveries in which not only is he the Ghost but also "he who played the Ghost" (p. 274). As W. O. and Eugene step along the sidewalks of the town, "a world frozen bare—a dead city of closed shops" (p. 271), Eugene's thoughts plunge to other deserted cities: "The Lost Atlantis. Ville d'Ys. The old lost towns, seasunken" (p. 276). In this mood Eugene gropes "for the doorless land of faery, that illimitable haunted country that opened somewhere below a leaf or a stone" (p. 277). His restless imagination may then have led him to dive deeper, but the misty images vanish with Gant's painful cry at the recurrence of his old illness. In this scene fantasy takes on a literary coloration, with figures from myth and motion pictures mingling haphazardly in a Joycean collage with such Altamont realities as Miss Bobbie Dukane at the Orpheum Theatre and Gorham's Undertaking Parlors.

For Eugene, only a few steps now remain before he is prepared for the creative act.

The ghost of course is the only agent through which return is possible; and without return, without moments of frozen time, or, Eugene thinks, without the concepts of time-past implicit in literary art, no artistic act is possible. In college Eugene seeks return through the reading of old books—*Sir Gawayne*, the *Book of Tobit*, Euripides (pp. 422-423) — but these old ghosts and spirits, such as the ghost of Hamlet's father, can find no home in "the ugly rolling land" (p. 423) of America where the university is situated. In America only the earth endures; no ghosts haunt the land. The meaning here, I presume, is the familiar complaint that America has no past upon which a traditional literature can be built. Eugene, even while reading Euripides, "walked, alone, a stranger," remembering his forebears in England, where all is "close and near." He thinks of how American hunger for return to such a literary past "makes us exiles at home, and strangers wherever we go" (p. 424).

Living in an America where it is ridiculous to conceive of the ghost of a Hamlet's Connecticut father walking "the night / Between Bloomington and Portland,

Maine" (p. 423), Eugene has to discover the return route of the ghost elsewhere, not in literature; and there are moments when, the pathways blocked as usual, his own ghost of the past haunts him. A typical example comes upon the occasion of his visit to a bawdy house in Exeter near the university where, upon going upstairs with the girl, he is censured by "the ghost, his stranger" (p. 409) for his intentional defection from paradisaic innocence. After the experience with the girl "his own lost ghost" haunts him; "he knew it to be irrecoverable" (p. 412).

Later, at work in Norfolk during the summer of his eighteenth year, Eugene is so cut away from his past that he feels as though he has died and been reborn. In this instance his prior life is synonymous with a state of preexistence. "All that had gone before lived in a ghostly world. He thought of his family, of Ben, of Laura James, as if they were ghosts. The world itself turned ghost" (p. 521). There in Norfolk beside "the everlasting sea" —customary symbol of unchanging, permanent nature and spirit—Eugene moves one step closer to the epiphany, and he is prompted to remember some of the other now-ghostlike personages he was in the past—the child at home, the newspaper carrier, the boy at the prostitute's—and he becomes "the ghost of his lost flesh" (p. 522). There remains, subsequently, only Ben's sacrificial death to propel Eugene toward the climactic return of the ghost.

But before any attempt is made to analyze that last chapter, in which both angel and ghost appear simultaneously, it is necessary to review the different angels of the novel. In the proem, where most of the major symbols are forecast, there is no mention of the angel; but in the first paragraph of the first chapter, as I have cited, "the proud coral cry of the cock" warns the ghost of the proem to depart, ushering in the Altamont day and focusing on "the soft stone smile of an angel" standing on

Gant's porch. Thenceforward until the end of the book, the angel is for daylight hours, and not for the darkness of preexistence, for the buried life, or for nighttime. Though the angel and the ghost in the novel differ in most ways, they are alike in recalling to man his alienation and isolation, his shortcomings and imperfections.

Wolfe is often erratic and inconsistent in the way he goes about using the ghost and the angel as symbolic commentary, and thus the singleness with which he employs W. O. Gant's angel is rare. Quite simply, Gant's angel stands for his ambition to be an artist; and its "silly" (p. 6), smiling, moronic stone face suggests that art, or so was it true for Gant, is unconcerned, unresponsive, unreasoning, and cold to the warm, impulsive advances of the young would-be creative man. Prior to his apprenticeship to a Baltimore stonecutter, W. O. had seen within a shop in the city "an angel poised upon cold phthisic feet, with a smile of soft stone idiocy" (p. 4). As he looked at the "angel with the carved stipe of lilystalk, a cold and nameless excitement possessed him. . . . He felt that he wanted, more than anything in the world, to carve delicately with a chisel. He wanted to wreak something dark and unspeakable in him into cold stone. He wanted to carve an angel's head." But by the end of his apprenticeship he had not yet learned to carve an angel's head. The dove, the lamb, the marble hands of death were within his power, "but not the angel" (p. 5). Even after settling in Altamont Gant had not quite given up his eagerness to become an artist and he had purchased, as a substitute for his yet unrealized aspiration, "the heavy simpering figure of an angel" (p. 17) to stand at the door of his shop, with other "grimy angels" inside. This angel is his tormentor, his accuser, his crown of thorns. He is excessively proud of it, but he publicly curses it and calls it a White Elephant and says he has been a fool to order it. Gant's zeal to consummate the creative act has left him restless and unsatisfied. His "hunger" to "own the earth," we read, led him "into new lands and toward the soft stone smile of an angel" (p. 70), meaning that the journeys of Gant the Far Wanderer are merely unfruitful movements towards accomplishment in art. Unfortunately for Gant art is never where he is, whether in Baltimore, or in the capital city of Old Catawba, or in Altamont. It always seems to elude him. Yet he loves his "ponderous fly-specked angels from Carrara in Italy which he bought at great cost, and never sold—they were the joy of his heart" (p. 99). Once again the fact that these angels come from Carrara stresses Wolfe's contention that creativity, for Gant, is not to be sought at home; and their fly-specked condition is proof that possibilities for Gant's artistic fulfillment are being constantly diminished by the fly-specks of life in Altamont. In 1912, when the Gant family holdings were being appraised, W. O.'s "stock of stones, monuments, and fly-specked angels represented an investment of $2,700" (p. 195), we are informed matter-of-factly, the inference being that art, no longer a gift to the spirit, now has for Gant a sordid market value. Several years later, when the angel on the porch with "its stupid white face" (p. 267) is sold to Queen Elizabeth for $420 to adorn the grave of a young prostitute, Gant's artistic impoverishment becomes total. Its purchase symbolizes the prostitution of his talent to a riotous and uncontrolled life, the ignominious end to a life-encompassing dream, and with its sale, "the angel leered vacantly down" (p. 268). In Gant's case art is the antithesis of the barrenness of life he has come to know. Artistic success would have freed him from the "incommunicable prison of this earth" and taught him "the great forgotten language." But Gant has neither the skill nor the stability to hammer out his vision.

Quite different from W. O.'s angel with its empty face wrought in cold marble is the airy, unsubstantial angel with whom Ben converses. In the speechless "prison of this earth," where no man can ever know his brother, Ben has discovered a comrade who understands him very well, and with derisive amusement he speaks to his angel about all the follies of earth's creatures. In this way he counteracts the horrid realities of Dixieland and Altamont. Ben has the ability to look upon people "with bitter clarity, [and he] answered their pretensions with soft mocking laughter, and a brief nod upwards and to the side to the companion to whom he communicated all his contemptuous observation—his dark satiric angel: 'Oh, my God! Listen to that, won't you?' " (p. 124). Such words are Ben's reaction to pompous or empty-headed statements, but particularly to Eliza's deceitfulness, affectations, and boastings. At other times, to indicate his delight when ostentation is ridiculed, Ben may withhold his words but he "laughed thinly to the Angel" (p. 174). On one occasion, when Eugene confides to Ben his illness after having been with a woman, Ben shouts at him, " 'Dry up! I don't want to hear about it. I'm not your damned Guardian Angel' " (p. 414). Of course the boy is taken to a doctor, but for Ben to have admitted that he was indeed Eugene's Guardian Angel would have altered the mute understanding between them. Ben's angel is a dark angel because Ben "walked alone in the darkness" (p. 112) and cannot find his way "into light and fellowship" (p. 113). There are times, too, when "death and the dark angels hovered" (p. 112) near him—for Ben is fated to die early—and Ben's special "dark angel wept [for him], but no one else saw, and no one knew" (p. 113). If Ben is caught in the bonds of flesh, not so the angel, a liberated spirit reminding Ben that the hour will come when he will be freed. Besides Ben only Eugene is aware of his brother's dark angel, and the boy vaguely senses that Ben's perceptiveness and truth, under other circumstances, might have been channeled into art. But the angel is dark, not bright, and art is the legacy Ben will pass on to Eugene.

As Ben lies dying, Eugene becomes frantic in his effort

to comprehend the nature of death. Wolfe writes in one of his most eloquent paragraphs that Eugene, trying to pray, is faced with the realization that he "did not believe in angels with soft faces and bright wings, but he believed in the dark spirits that hovered above the heads of lonely men. He did not believe in devils or angels, but he believed in Ben's bright demon to whom he had seen him speak so many times" (p. 556). Wolfe's symbolism in this passage is not clear to me, though I would hazard the guess that, as Ben's dark angel has always been his means of escape from man's folly, so now at this moment of mortality the "bright demon" will be his means of escape from "this most weary unbright cinder" (p. [2]). In the moonlit square of the last chapter Ben will make it possible for Eugene, whose struggles to "communicate" have been fruitless, to escape into art.

Different from the outgoing Gant with his intense drive to create, Ben is willing to retreat into a private dialogue with himself (his angel), and he makes no effort to fashion his subtle talents into art. Different, too, is the "wild angel" of Luke whose "coils and whorls of living golden hair" (p. 253) match his "demonic exuberance" at the time he is failing his college courses at Georgia Tech. And different is the "light" (p. 308) of Margaret Leonard, who, in teaching Eugene the glory and art of poetry, is "lost to the good angels."

Eugene's role is similar to his father's in that, unlike Ben's passive acceptance of life and his decision to remain with his dark angel and within himself, Eugene is constantly on the move searching for answers, traveling hither and thither, provoking the ghost into return, reading poetry, and listening for the angel's voice. Eugene's angel is mentioned only once—at a time when Eugene the searcher yearns to discover a pattern in life that will guarantee its endurance as art. "All of our life goes up in smoke," Eugene meditates. "There is no structure, no creation in it, not even the smoky structure of dreams. Come lower, angel; whisper in our ears. We are passing away in smoke. . . . How may we save ourselves?" (p. 295).

Here it is clear that if the ghost leads the way to the substance of art, it is the angel who moulds the raw substance into form. And how, Eugene questions, may we save ourselves? Salvation must come first through sacrifice, as in Christian doctrine, and second through the permanence of art.

Conclusive judgment on the angel and the ghost cannot be passed until Wolfe's original uncut last chapter is available for study. Kennedy reports that it was severely slashed before publication.[11] But even in the printed version it is a remarkable achievement. No reader seems ever to be affronted or disturbed that suddenly, without warning, Wolfe turns from thirty-nine chapters of realistic narrative technique to outright fantasy, in which time is frozen, a dead man speaks, the past is made present, and stone monuments move about.

On the morning of the day Eugene is to leave Altamont, at a quarter past three, Eugene comes into the square before his father's shop and there he meets with Ben "half-obscured in shadow" (p. 617). In response to Eugene's insistent questions, Ben vigorously denies that he is dead and therefore a ghost. Ben is right, of course, for this is fantasy, where ghosts are the normal way of things. Ben's spirit, not his body, is now alive. Everything is reversed, as is acceptable in dreams and fantasy. Within this episode of time suspended, in which that which is inanimate has life, it is Eugene who is the ghost, for only he is sentient. As the brothers talk, "the angel nearest Eugene moved her stone foot and lifted her arm to a higher balance. The slender lily stipe shook stiffly in her elegant cold fingers" (p. 618). Then, in conjunction with the revivi-

11. *The Window of Memory*, p. 176.

fication of the deceased Ben, other angels begin to walk "to and fro like huge wound dolls of stone ... the marble cherubim flew round and round" inside the shop, and "the carved lambs" give out "cold ewe-bleatings" (p. 620). Not yet trapped and postured securely within the trance, Eugene pauses long enough to wonder which one of them, Ben or himself, is the ghost. If Eugene is for a moment puzzled and startled by all these strange goings-on, not so Ben, for he now is as much angel as those suddenly vibrant winged statues. In short, the ghost has come back again, but as angel, not as ghost.

Chapter XL is the poetic account of a young man's transformation into artist. Ben the angel is once again Eugene's mentor—his Guardian Angel—though the cynical boy is not yet willing to believe that the sources of art are oneself, one's home. As the angels move about he shouts to Ben, who sees and approves, " 'Not here! Not here! ... It's not right, here! My God, this is the Square! There's the fountain! There's the City Hall! There's the Greek's lunch-room.' " In other words, there is Altamont; and art, so the unbelieving young man thinks, cannot be found at home, in Altamont. It can be found in Ville d'Ys, the city under the sea, or somewhere else, but not in commonplace Altamont. " 'In Babylon! In Thebes! In all the other places. But not here!' " (pp. 620-621). Ben's repeated assertion to Eugene that he is not a ghost annuls the boy's shrill cries.

As if to have the point reinforced, Eugene's eyes fall upon the Square, and there he beholds the myriad forms of himself and his brother. He sees "the fierce bright [no longer dark] horde of Ben ... in a thousand moments" (p. 622), and as he "watched the army of himself and Ben, which were not ghosts, and which were lost, he saw himself—his son, his boy, his lost and virgin flesh—come over past the fountain, leaning against the loaded canvas bag" and "he saw the lost child-face below the lumpy ragged cap." And as he looks, he calls out: " 'You! You! My son! My child! Come back! Come back!' "—hoping to freeze the moment so close in time to the preexistent state. Though the wraith of the boy vanishes, the Square still throngs "with their lost bright shapes" (p. 623).

For Eugene the crucial time has now come for answers. Where does one find oneself? Where is the happy land? Where is the end of hunger? The questions are hurled at Ben, who replies that there is no happy land outside oneself, no end of hunger, and as for oneself and the world, " '*You* are your world' " (p. 624), says Ben. Eugene, his soul " 'unimprisoned' " in this nimbus of animate angels, finally is forced into accepting Ben's dictum that all answers lie inside the artist, not without, and this knowledge will permit him to become creator. At daybreak, with Ben and the other visions faded away, "the angels on Gant's porch were frozen in hard marble silence" (p. 626), and the mountains around Altamont, which once had "rimmed in life" (p. 191), become "distant soaring ranges" (p. 626).

In this final chapter, without Ben's sacrificial death, there would have been no angel to spur Eugene to a search for answers. More than protector and guide, Ben is the spirit of Eugene's inner life, where all answers are. The dormant creative impulses within Eugene the artist are aroused not only with the return of Ben,[12] but also with the concurrent revitalization of W. O. Gant's stone angels, formerly as immobile and lifeless as W. O.'s unrealized aspirations. It is through both the sacrifice of his brother and the inheritance from his father that Eugene's life as artist is assured.

In looking for the reason why Wolfe chose *Look Homeward, Angel* as the title of his first novel, one can only surmise what went on in his mind. True, the three words were made up of the magic seventeen letters, but so were many other possible titles. And true, it was a beautiful,

12. W. P. Albrecht, in his "The Titles of *Look Homeward, Angel*," p. 57, also has this view.

lonely phrase, but then Wolfe was not unresourceful in
conjuring up beautiful, lonely phrases. It had the enchant-
ing word *angel* in it, and in fact many an angel lay within
the manuscript waiting for the moment of dramatic release. Certainly it is very doubtful that Wolfe chose the
words to emphasize close parallels between Milton's
poem and his own work. I do not agree with W. P. Albrecht that Eugene can be identified as Lycidas,[13] or that
we can discover a double for the weeping, elegy-writing
poet, nor do I think we can demonstrate effectively that the
angel of the title is W. O. Gant or Ben or Margaret Leonard or Eugene. More probable, I think, is that the choice
of title was prompted by its aptness in terms of what the
novelist had written in Chapter XL. As I see it, the speaker
of the imperative title is not Milton, not Eugene, not Ben,
not even necessarily Wolfe. The speaker is the omniscient
narrator of Eugene's first twenty years, a narrator who is
addressing Eugene and the novelist Wolfe himself (as
opposed to the story-teller of this particular novel). By
the end of the book the ghost has come back, no longer
lost and wind-grieved, but found and reclaimed. The angel
of the title, representing the artist in his active role and
therefore, prophetically and in extension, both Eugene and
Wolfe, is admonished not to look to the cosmic, the unknown, and the unfamiliar for those truths which it is the
duty of the artist to discover, but to look inward, land-
ward, homeward into the self. Though one may long for the
infinite and for recaptured glory, the quest for fulfillment,
and therefore for art, can be satisfied only within one's
self. Home is Altamont, one's own heart and spirit,
wherein lies the potency for artistic creation. Art is not
possible for everyone, not for the ill-qualified Gant, not
for the perceptive but passive Ben, and certainly not for

13. "Time as Unity in Thomas Wolfe," *New Mexico Quarterly
Review*, XIX (1949), 324. (Reprinted in *The Enigma*, pp. 239-248.)

worldly creatures like Eliza and Luke. We remember that it is only for Eugene that the angels come to life. And here it is that Milton's poem is relevant. Like St. Michael the angel of "the guarded mount," hopelessly looking outward over the watery wastes, the angel of Wolfe's first novel is cautioned to turn around and face a nearer reality.

So it is that *Look Homeward, Angel*, if viewed in terms of its two major symbols, is an investigation into the essentials of creativity. Though the distinction between the ghost and the angel is not always clearly marked, they have separate functions in establishing Wolfe's convictions about the nature of art. The ghost is the source, the brightness, the inspiration of art, and the ghost is ever available to him who is sensitive to its presence. Both ghost and angel are manifested in Ben, symbol of the sacrificial intermediary. The angel, initially figuring forth the education of the outsetting artist, is ultimately the permanence of art itself. If most men have their ghosts, not all have their angels, for not all men can perceive the "structure" without which "creation" (p. 295) is impossible. Only when both ghost and angel affirm themselves is man capable of the creative act.

The Discussion

MR. KENNEDY I would like to ask you to comment on a phrase that appears in the last chapter "*Et ego in Arcadia.*" Though you didn't get it in your paper, do you work this into your overall scheme?

MR. WALSER I didn't mention it in the paper, but I remember the phrase all right. I don't see why, as you say, it couldn't be worked into the overall scheme since I read the novel that way in my paper—as the sources and the ways that art operates. Certainly one thing that Wolfe makes very clear is that there was a source in literature, and isn't that what the phrase means? "And I have been in Arcadia." I assumed it to be a literary reference, and yet I think it could be discussed within the context of the last chapter. I was so busy with my ghosts and angels there that I didn't bring in all the sources of art again, although I had mentioned it earlier about the Connecticut Hamlet.

MR. KENNEDY You know how these things happen: you light on something that attracts your interest, and you think about it and you go one way and you go another, and I was curious as to what your response might be. I remember playing with this awhile, and being confused by the two interpretations of that phrase as it occurs and as it is used and interpreted in art and in world literature. There is a long article by Erwin Panofsky on what he calls the misuse of this phrase in art and literature, because he said it is a mistake to translate it "I, too, have lived in Arcadia" and he associates it with the painting, *Les Bergers d'Arcadie* by Nicolas Poussin, that shows the shepherds looking at the tomb, and on the tomb is written "Et ego in Arcadia." And he says that its meaning is "I, death, mortality, am also in Arcadia." Well, of course, when I read this article and I looked up Poussin's painting, I was led down the wrong path. I later discovered that in Wolfe's library there was a book with 1,000 famous quotations from classical literature, and I looked to see if *"Et ego in Arcadia"* was in there, and sure enough, it was; and it was translated as "I, too, have lived in Arcady," which is the way Goethe used it; and using it in a romantic sense, a nostalgic sense, it fits in very well with your reading of the last chapter, I think. Eugene learns at last that he has been living in a kind of place that is, in a way, Arcadia. Artistically he can use this; it is not anything to be ashamed of any more.

MR. WALSER   Thank you. I had not pursued the phrase in the way that you have.

MR. HUTTON   The idea of pattern in movement that you mentioned in your paper interested me because it seems that in the four major movements of the angel and the ghost that you talked about in *Look Homeward, Angel*, there is the first period of the lost eternity, signified by the mission bell, and so forth. Then there is a period of mechanical action which Eugene goes through, for example, where he wakes up, and there is a period when he is not asleep and he is not awake, and then he goes and delivers his papers. Then afterwards there is the period of tremendous realism after he finishes his paper route where he wakes up to the world; and this overlay on *Look Homeward, Angel* seems to travel through even into the last chapter, or especially in the last chapter, where you have a lost eternity and then a realism of distant hills and he is looking at something. Then you mentioned later that the ghostly exile of Eugene is a non-creative state, and he comes finally to realize that only the earth endures in America. Again there is a period of transition between eternity and realism. And the paper finishes with the awakening of the artist. Now the thing I'd like you to comment on is whether this is really what *Look Homeward, Angel* could be about—the final analysis of "I see eternity or I feel eternity and I finally wake up and am real," and is this what Eugene does and goes on to write?

MR. WALSER   You stated it beautifully; I find no quarrel at all. That was the way I began to see it in terms of these two symbols—I wasn't working with anything else. Remember that the exile is the source, but that is not the reality, ever. The exile is here now, but the angel is the one that has to fight for the reality of this state of exile, if it means anything at all. You say that he is constantly moving toward reality; the reality is the art itself—this

is the only reality. Everything else is unreal and imper-
manent, and the distant soaring ranges do become reality.
I thought of it in terms of the newspaperboy in limbo, and
then his going through the nimbus, for instance, and then
awakening into the real world; but it is an interesting and
wonderful way to look at the novel. I don't see why it
couldn't be worked out that way. I liked your comment.
I suggest that this is one of the wonderful numerous ways
that *Look Homeward, Angel* might be approached—moving from unreal to real, but then you have to define those
terms very carefully, because it seems to me that only art
is real as Eugene thinks about it; he is looking all over for
the pattern that will save him.

MR. DRAKE I thought your paper, especially at the end,
very illuminating and very wise in your refusal to work
out any sort of neat equation about who is the angel and
who is that, this, and the other, and what kind of context,
and the Wolfean context. It seems to me that the predominant note in the novel is extremely elegiac, and what the
novel gave to me was really one of the valid themes in
literature is the growing-up story; and isn't this a lament
meant for the dead Eugene and for the dead everybody,
in a sense?

MR. WALSER Any interpretation is possible, but I can
never find in Wolfe that this is what happens. This is
what Professor Albrecht said, you know: that Eugene is
wafted homeward and so forth and so on, but I tried to
make it clear at the beginning of my paper that all of this
information came out of *The Window of Memory*, because at the time that Wolfe wrote these things, at the
time he wrote the proem, at the times when he inserted
the "O lost, and by the wind grieved, ghost, come back
again," he didn't have those in there, isn't that right? He
went back later after he had written the lines and put
them here and here. I'm afraid I didn't come out very clear

on that. It is a novel of maturation, but it seems to me that Wolfe certainly has something in mind with this ghost and angel business that is all over the place, and if it is a novel of maturation, why can't it be simply a novel of artistic maturation? This is what I had in mind, and not the simple one of boy maturing from innocence and childhood into adulthood and sophistication, more or less the way that Sherwood Anderson . . .

MR. DRAKE What way would you care to pursue further the parallel to a portrait of the artist?

MR. WALSER They were rather parallel. I use the word maturation several times, and it is that because at the end Eugene has awakened—and because Wolfe uses the word unimprisoned after he had talked all 500 pages about being imprisoned. Then suddenly Eugene is unimprisoned, so something happened there: something escaped.

MR. HOLMAN How seriously do you take Wolfe's acceptance of the Wordsworthian idea of pre-existence?

MR. WALSER He never mentions birth, I don't think. If he ever mentions pre-existence, I don't recall it. But the parallels with the Wordsworth ode are just too startling, and I have tried to show how Stearns had started out, and I just take it on through to see if it wasn't something more than a theory. It is just bound to be; it is inescapable. I can't answer you because I don't think he ever uses the word.

MR. HOLMAN It seems to me that to a certain extent you are equating the ghost with the state of pre-existence, and therefore life and reality—to use these terms to describe actuality—are a growing imprisonment, so that the young boy from birth grows further and further away from this ghost. Then if art, represented by the angel, is the means whereby somehow we come back to some other statement of this order of things, are not the ghosts and the angels essentially performing the same function in the book, if the angel releases him as a mature person from the imprisonment that the flesh has given to his ghost?

MR. WALSER Both the ghost and the angel have something to do with the theory of the making of the artist. I don't know when Wolfe decided to let his novel be that sort of novel, but somewhere along the road, it seems to me, that this is what he had in mind—this is the point I was trying to make. It has something to do with the artist, but you brought up a very interesting point there that if the ghost is the source of art, then what did you say?

MR. HOLMAN The ghost is the essence, the source out of which the boy comes, what is lost and which he can never recover in the actual world. The angel then as art becomes a means of recovering a portion of this, and thus the ghost and the angel are in a sense a part of the same artistic matter.

MR. WALSER They are, and the only difference I attempted to make was that the ghost represents the raw materials of art and the angel was simply the means by which these raw materials could be chiseled into art itself. Remember that I said at one point—and I put that remark in there very carefully—that Wolfe is quite inconsistent and just when you think you have got the angel and ghost nailed, he is off talking about Ben's dark angel, and then that is something else again, almost entirely; and if you try to put a definition on the angel and this is what it means everytime, then of course you are in bad trouble, because the novel cannot be read that way. Some of the forty-seven angels and eighty-six ghosts have no relationship to any symbols at all. Rhetorical rather than symbolic. The only time Eugene's angel is mentioned is when he says, "Come lower, angel; whisper in our ears. . . . How may we save ourselves?" That passage is so revealing as to what Wolfe was feeling at the time: he was trying to show that Eugene was trying to discover a pattern, a structure for art. I would happily eliminate, from such a paper as this, Ben's dark ghost. I had a terrible time trying to work that into some artistic connection, but it seemed to me that it did fit eventually. But this is what we all do: we begin to write a paper and we make it all fit.

MR. SINGH I think we are probably not giving adequate attention to the departures from this romantic laconic theory of the soul in Wordsworthian philosophy. Wordsworth speaks of "trailing clouds of glory," but on the contrary, Wolfe talks of "Naked and alone." In looking around his novels for a definition of the spirit, I found a most valuable description in the chapter about the death of his father, in which he describes the massive sculptured hands of his dead father. You think the spirit of the man was summed up in those hands. And he defines it as some energy that persists, not an intangible substance, but something that expresses itself in action, in character, in destiny. This is a very simple view of the spirit, and this is consistent with his view of eternity—not as a timeless order but just an extension of time. Whenever he refers to eternity he does not refer to it in philosophical terms, but as the eternity of hills and mountains and rivers.

MR. KENNEDY Mr. Singh, I think that you are overemphasizing something, because both of these kinds of eternity are in *Look Homeward, Angel*, and what is more, they seem to be somewhat in conflict. This is, I suppose you might say, in some ways what Eugene discovers at the end of the book—that the kind of ordinary life in Altamont that he has lived has its place on the enduring earth that abides forever, whereas he has perhaps been too attracted to the attempt to achieve a state of timelessness, or something of that sort, that his romantic yearning has expressed. However, the only thing I wanted to add to your comment was the fact that both of these things are here, and as for Wolfe's using Wordsworth's view of pre-existence (and Wordsworth didn't believe in it himself) Wolfe translated Plato's *Phaedo* when he was a sophomore or freshman at the University of North Carolina; and anyone who has translated Plato's *Phaedo* from the original Greek has gone to the source beyond Wordsworth. I think some of this got reawakened with his study of the romantic poets at Harvard, but there is a real Platonic reaching back to the original theory that he had. And as I say, I think both of these are there, and are there in conflict.

MR. SINGH I think the accent on pre-existence derives from the fact that immortality is defined as the continuity of human life, active life, collective life from generation to generation, and this idea of the ghost and the angel is very ingenious, but perhaps not very accurate. These things, I think, can probably relate to his theory of time in which we are living the present moment but pushed by the past. Now the ghost often represents this pressure of the past, that which is dead and gone but continues to influence the present; and the angels are the dreams, the future that is always beckoning to us, and leading us on. The longing to be a great artist is again symbolized by the angels.

MR. WALSER I would like to inject something. In the first place, I am no more sure than you are that Wolfe believed in pre-existence any more than Wordsworth did. It seems to me to be a part of the source of art: it is what's inside; it's what was there to begin with; it is what is in each person in this room, and how are you going to get the perfect thing out of self, enclosed as it is within this strange body of ours in which we are imprisoned? I don't think Wolfe believed in Platonic pre-existence and souls floating around, but it was necessary that it be the home, the inside, the beginning; and this is where art was, and the whole allegory, the whole symbolism, begins to work from this. Wolfe, it is true, doesn't trouble himself on the perfect heavenly pre-existence; he is only concerned with what is with the stranger at the moment of birth. It becomes a dreadful, dreary, dark thing, and then how are you going to get this dreary dark thing to be bright; it's only through art and creation—he doesn't emphasize with Wordsworth the trailing clouds of glory—he is concerned only with time.

Another point that you made about the hands of W. O. Gant even in death—this seemed to me to be in *Look Homeward, Angel* long before that passage in *Of Time and the River* was busy with the angel symbol, saying that he had all of this inside but never the angel to bring it out. This may have resulted from many things, as I said—in his uncontrolled life and the way he corrupted himself when he kept on trying to fight it; but never for one minute does it seem to me that *Look Homeward, Angel* does not argue that the making of an artist is an inherited thing and that Eugene inherited his father's urge for art and that this was a very important thing to this whole familiar process here—of the brother's sacrifice and the father's urging coming together and there you have the artist. The man who writes books, Eugene or George Webber it was to be eventually, the artist is a man who finds a meaning, a balance, and a purpose in life—isn't that what it is? And you can't always do that, and this is what he was trying to do. Wolfe was trying to tell us as truthfully as he could, with a young romantic mind as he had at the time he wrote the book, how it seemed to him. Later on, as we all know, he repudiated the total Eugene Gantian stuff, and he said it was all bad, and he wasn't going to have any more to do with that, but Wolfe was wrong—this was the great thing that he did.

MR. SINGH Was Wolfe trying to describe Eugene at the moment of birth as a spark of the divine separated from some essence? No. He described Eugene as being born at the spirit of time—the summation of all world history.

MR. PAYNE One brief question. You gave an account of sometimes the ghost appearing and sometimes the angel appearing, but isn't your point which we are talking about that Ben is a sacrifice? I grant you that it makes sense to the reader of the novel, but is it in some way textually substantiated?

MR. WALSER I simply could not put my finger on sacrifice in the book any more than I could on pre-existence. I'm afraid that is just my reading of it, and it seems to be supported by a number of critics. I don't see how we can avoid it. Otherwise why bring Ben back as the ghost-angel in Chapter XL unless he is the sacrificial victim so that somebody else may live. In a sense, he has the answer, but he can't do it—"I give up my life, so you can do it." It seems like the Christlike-cross business to me.

MR. REEVES Well, it is bound to be Christlike-cross business, because Wolfe was reared in the Presbyterian church, and he was heir to the Christian heritage. He was also thoroughly indoctrinated with the Wordsworthian idea, and I think he shaped the materials that he had, and he had some urge during his creation of Look Homeward, Angel to use the familiar and to touch the familiar at various points and degrees. Now how much of it was conscious and how much was unconscious, I don't know, and I don't know that anyone else knows, but I think it is characteristic of all great writers that they put more into their work than they realize they are doing.

MR. KENNEDY Do you associate the angel that Ben speaks to with the spirit of his twin brother Grover at all?

MR. WALSER   I never did, but by jove it is worth a whole argument.

MR. KENNEDY   The reason I brought this up was you remember in that quotation I was reading last night from the phrases, and Wolfe stopped at one little place. The punctuation doesn't show, the way I was reading it, but there is a little place where he has got parentheses and he asks the question: "What's it like to have a twin—did Ben go through life with this brooding fatality with him?" This, plus some references in the text, made me associate the twin, the dead twin, with the figure to whom Ben speaks.

MR. WALSER   I wish I had thought that up. I had the worst problem in this paper with Ben's angel. It just didn't seem to fit. Where did you find this? Is it in *Look Homeward, Angel?*

MR. KENNEDY   No, it's in the Autobiographical Outline, the one Wolfe prepared for writing *Look Homeward, Angel.*
    One more thing that I just must say about Mr. Walser's paper—the thought that he provoked, the feeling that he provoked in me: I was very much struck, and I think possibly some others here must have been, by some of the things that he was saying in connection with the timelessness of art and by the fact that Fred Wolfe was sitting right over here, someone who lived through these materials with his brother a long time ago, but here we are talking about this artistic object, the product that Thomas Wolfe created—it really is timeless.

C. Hugh Holman

Thomas Wolfe:
Rhetorical Hope and
Dramatic Despair

Thomas Wolfe was the master of two distinct modes of writing—although there are unkind critics, such as Bernard De Voto, who would say that he was mastered by them. One of these modes is that of rhetoric; the other is that of dramatic rendering. By rhetoric is meant the direct statement of ideas and emotions in language designed to persuade the reader. In fiction it is the substitution of the description of emotion for the evocation of emotion. On the other hand, dramatic rendering presents characters and actions and makes its appeal through the feelings they evoke. This distinction was in Henry James's mind when he defined the "sign of the born novelist" as being "a respect unconditioned for the freedom and vitality, the absoluteness when summoned, of the creatures he invokes," and contrasted it to "the strange and second-rate policy of explaining or presenting them by reprobation or apology—of taking the short cuts and anticipating the emotions and judgments about them that should be left, at the best, to the perhaps not most intelligent reader."[1]

1. "Ivan Turgenieff," *Library of the World's Best Literature* (1897), reprinted in *The Portable Henry James*, ed. M. D. Zabel (New York, 1968), p. 457.

The two are often fundamentally incompatible, but when they are used to re-enforce each other they can function with great strength. Contrast, for example, these two selections from *Of Time and the River*. In the first the dying W. O. Gant is talking with his wife:

> "Eliza,"—he said—and at the sound of that unaccustomed word, a name he had spoken only twice in forty years—her white face and her worn brown eyes turned toward him with the quick and startled look of an animal —"Eliza," he said quietly, "you have had a hard life with me, a hard time. I want to tell you that I'm sorry."
> And before she could move from her white stillness of shocked surprise, he lifted his great right hand and put it gently down across her own.[2]

The second selection is a meditation on Gant's death as it affects his son Eugene. Although it runs on for several pages, the opening is typical:

> October had come again, and that year it was sharp soon: frost was early, burning the thick green on the mountain sides to massed brilliant hues of blazing colors, painting the air with sharpness, sorrow and delight—and with October. Sometimes, and often, there was warmth by day, an ancient drowsy light, a golden warmth and pollenated haze in afternoon, but over all the earth there was the premonitory breath of frost, an exultancy for all the men who were returning, a haunting sorrow for the buried men, and for all those who were gone and would not come again.
> His father was dead, and now it seemed to him that he had never found him. His father was dead, and yet he sought him everywhere, and could not believe that he was dead, and was sure that he would find him. It was October and that year, after years of absence and of wandering, he had come home again.[3]

In these passages Wolfe writes of the same fundamental situation—and of one of his major themes, death. In the first he writes as a novelist and in the second as a prose poet. But this mixed style bothers us relatively little, for the rhetorical passage extends and universalizes the particular incident that is presented with objective force in the first selection. The notebooks—ably edited by Richard S. Kennedy and Paschal Reeves—contain ample evidence that such prose poems—and this one in particular—were sketched out independent of their later use.[4] But this fact is ultimately of little significance, for however he came to write them first, in his early books Wolfe usually wedded these rhetorical passages effectively to their final dramatic context.

At the opening of Book VII of *Of Time and the River,* there is a much less certain union of scene and rhapsody. This is the section that begins:

> Play us a tune on an unbroken spinet, and let the bells ring, let the bells ring!...Waken the turmoil of forgotten streets, let us hear their sounds again unmuted, and unchanged by time, throw the light of Wednesday morning on the Third Crusade, and let us see Athens on an average day.[5]

This famous passage is an attempt to impose the themes of time and the quest for the father on material in which they are not necessarily apparent. In other words, here rhetoric is not re-enforcing dramatic scene but is being used as a substitute for it. And the problem is further complicated by the fact that in the passage on October and death, the brooding rhetoric is Eugene's and thus has a kind of dramatic propriety, while in the passage on the unbroken spinet the rhetoric seems to be the expression of some undefined auctorial persona who differs from Eugene, and who is, in fact, commenting on the protagonist's experience. The temptation is strong to say that

---

4. *The Notebooks of Thomas Wolfe,* ed. Richard S. Kennedy and Paschal Reeves, 2 vols. (Chapel Hill, 1970).

5. *Of Time and the River,* p. 853.

Wolfe as recorder of the conversation of Gant and Eliza is working as a novelist, and that Wolfe evoking music from the unbroken spinet is indulging in direct self-expression.

Such mixed materials as these run throughout Wolfe's work. For example, in *Look Homeward, Angel,* after the magnificent scene between Eugene and Laura, in which Wolfe's poetic style seems perfectly attuned to the ecstasy of the young love which he is describing, he suddenly shifts in time and in point of view to declare, "Come up into the hills, O my young love. Return! O lost, and by the wind grieved, ghost, come back again, as first I knew you in the timeless valley."[6] The mixed modes and the mixed time perspectives (who is speaking and when?) render one of Wolfe's most impressive poetic expressions novelistically questionable.

That Wolfe should have felt no compulsion to synthesize these elements is not suprising, for he seems to define reality in terms of negations, to deal in oppositions, to be unable to bring forth any idea without setting against it a contradiction. And he seems, too, to have a confident faith that the synthesis of these opposites is a consistent function of reality itself, that it inevitably happens and does not need his guiding hand. Thus he can shift from scene to exhortation, from action to explanation, from immediacy to nostalgic perspective without sensing that he is doing primary violence to his view of the world.[7] The result is that his books consist of segments written in different styles and contrasting modes. Thus he produces works which, if judged in the terms of Northrop Frye's definitions of genres,[8] are mixtures of

6. *Look Homeward, Angel* (New York, 1929), p. 456.

7. I have discussed this aspect of Wolfe's work at length in my essay "Thomas Wolfe" in *Seven Modern American Novelists,* ed. William Van O'Connor (Minneapolis, 1964), pp. 189-225.

8. *Anatomy of Criticism* (Princeton, 1957).

two or three fictional modes, or in Mr. Kennedy's term are fictional thesauruses.

The tendency for these modes to be separate rather than re-enforcing increases very much in the posthumous novels, despite the fact that Edward Aswell assembled them from manuscript material and in so doing exercised great freedom in excision, re-arrangement, and even re-writing on occasion. Of course, acting against Aswell's attempt to achieve unity through editing was the circumstance of his having to work with a vast and very fragmentary and incomplete manuscript. In *You Can't Go Home Again,* the book in which I wish to examine Wolfe's use of these two modes, we have a very loosely-constructed work whose unity seems to reside primarily in the presence of George Webber as a registering personality upon whom a variety of experiences make their impact. To a lesser extent than in any of the three preceding novels, this protagonist is not an actor in the dramas that he witnesses. He is a minor participant, not a major figure, in most of the episodes in the novel.

In this respect *You Can't Go Home Again* is markedly similar to the work of Herman Melville—a writer to whom Wolfe's debts have not been given their full deserts. In fact, structurally there are remarkable parallels between the works of the two men. Melville's protagonists are usually minor actors in his works, and the dramatic action is centered on other characters whom the protagonist observes. The weight of interpretation rests upon this almost passive but observing narrator and is more a function of style and metaphysical conceit than of action. This characteristic is obvious in *Moby-Dick,* where from time to time Ishmael almost becomes Emerson's "transparent eyeball," through whom we view Captain Ahab and his quest. Yet Ishmael comes from the voyage of the Pequod having learned not Ahab's course but the error of it. A similar role is played by Redburn, by White-Jacket, and by Taji in *Mardi* (although Melville apparently gives the final answer to Babbalanja in that work). When Melville, in *Pierre,* shifts from the first person discursive narrator to the third person many of the difficulties which we also encounter in Wolfe appear, including the great problem of distinguishing between the attitudes held by Pierre Glendenning and those held by the author. The result is that *Pierre* is often called autobiographical in a derogatory sense. Wolfe's effort to use a first person narrator in *Of Time and the River*—an effort defeated by his publishers—would have resolved the similar problem in this work to a substantial extent. *You Can't Go Home Again* would also have benefited very much from first person narration, and, indeed, the last section shifts to the first person, but so late that the impression is that it is Wolfe speaking directly rather than George Webber.

You Can't Go Home Again consists in large part of materials originally written as self-contained units— "Boom Town," "The World That Jack Built," and "I Have a Thing to Tell You!" As a result sections like Books III and IV and the conclusion, where the hortatory and rhetorical voice of the author, either thinly disguised as George Webber or in several cases not disguised at all, are more different in mode from the dramatic than such passages had been in the earlier novels. The inclination is to say that in fact in their present form such passages are not representative of their author's intentions—as indeed Hamilton Basso declared upon the publication of the book[9] and many others, including Richard S. Kennedy,[10] have noted since. But I fear that that is letting Wolfe off a little more easily than we are justified in doing. There are, in fact, two thematic elements in the novel—thematic

9. Review of *You Can't Go Home Again, New Republic,* September 23, 1940.
10. *The Window of Memory* (Chapel Hill, 1962), pp. 403-411.

elements that are not truly congenial—and each is expressed in a distinctly different stylistic mode, so that we can with some justice say that *You Can't Go Home Again* is a mixture of rhetorical hope and dramatic despair. The rhetorical passages and the dramatic scenes in *You Can't Go Home Again* differ from the earlier books also in subject matter. In this novel what Webber does and thinks matters less than what he sees: hence there is a much stronger social content in the action of the book. And the rhetorical sections, which in the earlier books had elaborated upon the emotions surrounding events as the "timeless valley" section does in *Look Homeward, Angel*, tend here to express more abstract attitudes about the social world, as the famous "Credo" that closes the novel does.

The increasing presence of these disparate elements is to a large degree the result, I think, of Wolfe's growing concern with the outer world and its problems, a concern that led him to the frequent use of a kind of incident that appears only occasionally in the earlier works. Late in December 1937, less than nine months before his death, he wrote his new editor Edward Aswell:

> ...like many other young men, I began life as a lyrical writer. I am no longer a very young man—I am thirty-seven years old—and I must tell you that my vision of life has changed since I began to write about ten years ago, and that I shall never again write the kind of book that I wrote then. Like other men, I began to write with an intense and passionate concern with the designs and purposes of my own youth; and like many other men, that preoccupation has now changed to an intense and passionate concern with the designs and purposes of life.[11]

The life which had impressed itself hauntingly upon his mind during the years of his maturity, it must be

11. *The Letters of Thomas Wolfe,* ed. Elizabeth Nowell (New York, 1956), p. 700.

remembered, was the life of depression-stricken America. He knew it through the suffering of his own family in Asheville, a suffering which he portrayed in the last five chapters of the first book and in chapters 25 and 26 of *You Can't Go Home Again*; and he knew it through direct observation in Brooklyn and Manhattan. In *The Story of a Novel* he is very explicit about what he saw in New York during the depression:

> Everywhere around me . . . I saw the evidence of an incalculable ruin and suffering. My own people, the members of my own family had been ruined, had lost all the material wealth and accumulation of a lifetime. . . . And that universal calamity had somehow struck the life of almost everyone I knew. Moreover, in this endless quest and prowling of the night through the great web and jungle of the city, I saw, lived, felt, and experienced the full weight of that horrible human calamity.
>
> I saw a man whose life had subsided into a mass of shapeless and filthy rags, devoured by vermin; wretches huddled together for a little warmth in freezing cold squatting in doorless closets upon the foul seat of a public latrine within the very shadow, the cold shelter of palatial and stupendous monuments of wealth. I saw acts of sickening violence and cruelty, the menace of brute privilege, a cruel and corrupt authority trampling ruthlessly below its feet the lives of the poor, the weak, the wretched, and the defenseless of the earth.[12]

And these things are in large measure the chief subjects of the episodes that make up *You Can't Go Home Again*. They are realized in the syphilitic Judge Rumford Bland, preying like some dark angel of wickedness upon the poor and underprivileged of Libya Hill; in the insanity of the real estate boom and the pain that follows the pricking of its bubble; in the contrast of rich luxury and the life of the poor upon which that luxury exists in "The World That Jack Built"; in the faceless C. Green whose suicidal plunge from the twelfth floor of the Admiral Francis

12. *The Story of a Novel* (New York, 1936), pp. 59-60.

Drake Hotel is for one brief moment a matter of attention if not of concern to his fellowmen; and in the agony of Hitler's Third Reich, where all the implications of these things come shockingly to life at the touch of absolute evil in the person of "The Dark Messiah."

But there is another aspect of Wolfe's work which can best be understood if we contrast him with John Dos Passos, a writer with whom social historians often link him as a novelist of the 1930s, deeply concerned with the quality of experience in that anguished decade. Such a comparison is apt, for both writers attempted to imprison a record of American life in long and ambitious works with many formal oddities, works that can be called novels only if the term is loosely used. Henry Steele Commager has said that "Dos Passos was the most social minded of the major novelists" between the two world wars and that "Thomas Wolfe's quarrel with his society remained ... personal and ... artistic."[13] But the differences go deeper than this. Dos Passos belonged, as Alfred Kazin has recently noted, to "those American writers from the upper class, born on the eve of our century ... (who) were brought up in ... the last stable period in American history"[14] and whose dreams of an admirable order were betrayed by the First World War, so that they left its battlefields, where they had been ambulance drivers and Red Cross workers, with a profound sense of disillusionment. Wolfe, on the other hand, was born into a middle-middle class family in which his personal security seemed threatened by intense domestic schisms, with the result that, despite an overly possessive mother, he appeared always to have seen himself as alone and defenseless.[15] Furthermore, he grew up in a small southern

13. *The American Mind* (New Haven, 1951), pp. 267-269.

14. "John Dos Passos: Inventor in Isolation," *Saturday Review,* March 15, 1969, p. 17.

15. See, for example, *Letters of Thomas Wolfe,* pp. 370-371.

provincial city, imbibed from his closest companions—the books he read—most of the ideals of a standard middle-class world, was educated in a state university which he regarded as a wilderness outpost of "great Rome," and was too young to participate in the war, which—like many young middle-class sixteen- and seventeen-year-olds of the time—he romanticized as the last great chivalric crusade.

Furthermore, the long years of introspection which culminated in the lyrical *Look Homeward, Angel* pretty effectively shut him off—except for fairly superficial satire of the Sinclair Lewis type—from a critical examination of the postulates of middle-class America. He vigorously declared himself not to be of the "Lost Generation,"[16] and could, on occasion, in letters and elsewhere, attack the critics of American life with all the pride of a Rotarian and the unquestioning energy of the provincial.[17] When, in the loneliness of Europe, he discovered that America was his subject, the America he discovered was still tied for him in powerful ways to the nineteenth-century dream which had gone up in the holocaust of the world war for writers like John Dos Passos, Ernest Hemingway, E. E. Cummings, and Edmund Wilson.

Hence, to the end, Wolfe held firmly to a belief in America that was of a different dimension and quality from that of his contemporaries, while he portrayed in telling detail in his pictures of the life around him many of the assumptions and despairs of the depression world he inhabited. He once declared in a letter to a friend that "I seem to have been born a Freshman—and in many ways I'm afraid I'll continue to be one."[18] Expressed another way, Wolfe moved physically and artistically out

16. See *Thomas Wolfe's Purdue Speech: "Writing and Living,"* ed. William Braswell and Leslie A. Field (Purdue University, 1964), pp. 36-37.

17. See *The Letters of Thomas Wolfe to His Mother,* ed. C. Hugh Holman and Sue Fields Ross (Chapel Hill, 1968), p. 94.

18. *Letters of Thomas Wolfe,* pp. 192-193.

into the great world of Boston, New York, and Europe, but he remained a sojourner rather than a native, a spectator rather than a participant, an observer rather than a true believer in the postulates of this larger world he inhabited for most of his adult life. Hence he brought the childlike vision of experience continuingly to bear on a steadily widening world, and therein lay one of his greatest powers; but he also brought to bear on the complexities of commitment in that larger world the simpler and uninstructed faith of the Populist democracy in which his social and political being had been nurtured. What he saw and what he believed came into increasingly tormented conflict, and he neither felt the need nor had the time in which to reconcile them. But he did have two methods of writing which allowed him in the late years to do a kind of justice to both vision and belief. That they rent the ideological fabric of his work would, I think, have bothered him relatively little.

Again the contrast with John Dos Passos is illuminating. In *U.S.A.* Dos Passos attempted to make the dynamics of history in his time the fundamental structure of his work, and he brought to it fresh and complex techniques—the Newsreels, the case histories of fictional representative Americans, and the biographical sketches of real persons who embodied common beliefs or attitudes. Along with these objective treatments Dos Passos included another mode of statement, "The Camera Eye," which gives us a lyrical and intense expression of the author's attitudes and emotions at the time of the action of the story. The Camera Eye sections are not fixed in some later time; they record the growing disillusionment of the author, as he encounters a world of widening experience. He moves from the child's view in "The Camera Eye (7)" which ends:

we clean young American Rover Boys handy with tools Deerslayers played hockey Boy Scouts and cut figure eights

> on the ice. Achilles Ajax Agamemnon I couldn't learn to
> skate and kept falling down[19]

to the despair of "The Camera Eye (50)" which begins "they have clubbed us off the streets   they are stronger they are rich" and reaches the ultimate expression of rejection in:

> all right we are two nations
> America our nation has been beaten by strangers who
> have bought the laws and fenced off the meadows and cut
> down the woods for pulp and turned our pleasant cities
> into slums and sweated the wealth out of our people.[20]

Wolfe presented dramatic pictures of that same world, pictures which portrayed it in terms not significantly different from those of Dos Passos. But Wolfe's are drawn not objectively by experimental methods but directly as the experience of his increasingly faceless protagonist. When the author Wolfe wishes to speak, he does so directly, and from time to time we are confused as to whether he intends his remarks to be comments on the protagonist's experience or comments by the protagonist. These rhetorical comments reflect Wolfe's relatively static view and are seemingly fixed in the present rather than the time of action of the book. If we use Dos Passos's metaphor, we can say the lens setting of Wolfe's camera eye undergoes surprisingly little adjustment as the book progresses.

I suppose this is what Robert Penn Warren was talking about when he penned his famous wisecrack about Wolfe: " ... it may be well to recollect that Shakespeare merely wrote Hamlet; he was not Hamlet."[21] But that remark is

19. *U.S.A.: 42nd Parallel* (New York, 1937), p. 81.

20. *U.S.A.: The Big Money* (New York, 1937), pp. 461-463.

21. "The Hamlet of Thomas Wolfe," in *The Enigma of Thomas Wolfe,* ed. Richard Walser (Cambridge, Mass., 1953), p. 132.

actually more scintillating than sensible; for the genres in which the two are working are radically dissimilar. Wolfe *did* choose both to play Hamlet and to write it, for his great subject was the impact of the world on a protagonist frankly quite like himself. In Shakespeare's play there is action and there is rhetoric; the action is Shakespeare's presentation of Hamlet's world; the rhetoric is Hamlet's (and others') interpretation of that world. I suppose what bothers us about *You Can't Go Home Again* is that what George Webber sees and what happens to him is very much like Hamlet's description of the world as

> an unweeded garden,
> That grows to seed; things rank and gross in nature
> Possess it merely.[22]

Yet many of his remarks about it, his rhetorical flourishes, smack a little too much of Polonius—or, to be fairer, of Walt Whitman evoking the spirit of America and its promise.

It is significant, I think, that when Wolfe, in *The Story of a Novel*, describes the growth of the impulse that led him to see America as his proper subject, that launched him on an artistic effort that has marked similarities to that of the epic poet, he assigns the motive force to loneliness and a haunting sense of loss. This occurred in Europe, and Wolfe says, "I discovered America during these years abroad out of my very need of her. The huge gain of this discovery seemed to come directly from my sense of loss."[23] And he adds a little later, "Now my memory was at work night and day, in a way that I could at first neither check nor control and that swarmed unbidden in a stream of blazing pageantry across my mind,

22. *Hamlet, Prince of Denmark*, I, ii, 135-137.
23. *The Story of a Novel*, pp. 30-31.

with the million forms and substances of the life that I had left, which was my own, America."[24] In a sense, then, the substance of Wolfe's work was America recollected in nostalgia. Even *You Can't Go Home Again* primarily describes events that occurred in 1929 and 1930 (the German episode is later but it is unique in this respect), but he views them from the vantage point of a later time. Indeed, Wolfe's whole concept of time in the novel required that a sense of the past and the present commingle against an awareness of eternity: thus he shares with Dos Passos a great interest in time and history, but in his case it is history viewed more philosophically than socially.

In *You Can't Go Home Again* Wolfe skillfully uses the novelist's basic tool, character, to portray his world and its corruption. Judge Rumford Bland, whom everyone instinctively knew to be evil, is a microcosmic representation of the town of Libya Hill. Randy Shepperton is the average American caught in the depression, and Wolfe is very explicit about it. He says, "Behind Randy's tragedy George thought he could see a personal devil in the form of a very bright and plausible young man, oozing confidence and crying, 'Faith!' when there was no faith. . . . And it seemed to George that Randy's tragedy was the essential tragedy of America."[25] Mr. Jack epitomizes the capitalistic system, and again Wolfe is explicit: Mr. Jack enjoyed, he said, "the privilege of men selected from the common run because of some mysterious intuition they were supposed to have." And he added, " . . . it seemed to Mr. Jack . . . not only entirely reasonable but even natural that the whole structure of society from top to bottom should be honeycombed with privilege and dishonesty."[26] Amy Carleton, rich millionairess of many marriages and

24. Ibid., pp. 31-32.
25. *You Can't Go Home Again* (New York, 1940), pp. 395-396.
26. Ibid., p. 189.

of total moral collapse, symbolizes the decay of high society. Wolfe writes, "It seemed, therefore, that her wealth and power and feverish energy could get her anything she wanted ... [But] The end could only be destruction, and the mark of destruction was already apparent upon her."[27] And C. Green was a type of all the nameless, faceless people who are the victims of an inhuman system in an unseeing city. Of him Wolfe declared:

> He was life's little man, life's nameless cipher, life's manswarm atom, life's American—and now he lies disjected and exploded on a street in Brooklyn!
> He was a dweller in mean streets ... a man-mote in the jungle of the city, a resident of grimy steel and stone, a mole who burrowed in rusty brick.[28]

And the indictment does not stop with people, but extends to descriptions of scenes and actions. Of a hill in Libya Hill he writes:

> It had been one of the pleasantest places in the town, but now it was gone. An army of men and shovels had advanced upon this beautiful green hill and had leveled it down to an ugly flat of clay, and had paved it with a desolate horror of white concrete, and had built stores and office buildings and parking spaces—all raw and new.[29]

"The town of his childhood," he declared, "was changed past recognition.... It looked like a battlefield, cratered and shell-torn with savage explosions of brick, cement, and harsh new stucco."[30]

Nazi Germany, with its old dark evil, comes finally to symbolize for him the end of the path on which America also is traveling. "It was," he says, "a picture of the Dark

27. Ibid., p. 249.
28. Ibid., pp. 467-468.
29. Ibid., p. 111.
30. Ibid., p. 145.

Ages come again—shocking beyond belief, but true as the hell that man forever creates for himself."[31] And he adds, "I realized fully, for the first time, how sick America was, and saw, too, that the ailment was akin to Germany's —a dread world-sickness of the soul."[32] This condition of sickness strikes George Webber with a sense of profound disillusionment. Wolfe declares:

> To find man's faith betrayed and his betrayers throned in honor, themselves the idols of his bartered faith! To find truth false and falsehood truth, good evil, evil good, and the whole web of life so changing, so mercurial!
> It was so different from the way he had once thought it would be—and suddenly, convulsively, forgetful of his surroundings, he threw out his arms in an instinctive gesture of agony and loss.[33]

This despair comes to one who, Wolfe says, knew "that if he was ever to succeed in writing the books he felt were in him, he must turn about and lift his face up to some nobler height."[34] For Wolfe the writers of his time were people each of whom "had accepted part of life for the whole . . . some little personal interest for the large and all-embracing interest of mankind." And Webber asked himself, "If that happened to him, how, then, could he sing America?"[35]

Yet sing America Wolfe did. In spite of all he saw about him, he remained more totally committed to the nineteenth-century American dream of an egalitarian society than any other major novelist of this century, and at place after place in his novels he employed his great gift for poetic language to create ringing assertions of hope for the success of that democracy. A part of that faith was

31. Ibid., p. 728.
32. Ibid., pp. 729-730.
33. Ibid., p. 263.
34. Ibid., p. 321.
35. Ibid., pp. 262-263.

a still unshaken belief in man himself. In a long section, "The Locusts Have No King," he writes:

> This is man: for the most part a foul, wretched, abominable ... hater of his kind, a cheater, a scorner, a mocker, a reviler, a thing that kills and murders in a mob or in the dark.
> [But] Behold his works:
> He needed speech to ask for bread—and he had Christ! He needed songs to sing in battle—and he had Homer! ... He needed walls and a roof to shelter him—so he made Blois! ... It is impossible to scorn this creature. For out of his strong belief in life, this puny man made love. At his best, he *is* love. Without him there can be no love, no hunger, no desire.[36]

And he extends this faith to America in one of his two or three best known passages and one that is in a very Whitmanesque context, that of being seated at night on the hackles of the Rocky Mountains and looking to East and West and thus gaining a vast continental vision. He concludes:

> So, then, to every man his chance—to every man, regardless of his birth, his shining, golden opportunity—to every man the right to live, to work, to be himself and to become whatever thing his manhood and his vision can combine to make him—this, seeker, is the promise of America.[37]

Even in these ecstatic moments, he is not blind or forgetful of the dark canker at the heart of his native land, but this evil is an enemy whose triumph is unthinkable to Wolfe: "I think," he says, "the enemy is here before us, too. But I think we know the forms and faces of the enemy, and in the knowledge that we know him, and shall meet him, and eventually must conquer him is also our living hope."[38]

36. Ibid., pp. 434-436.
37. Ibid., p. 508.
38. Ibid., p. 741.

His final judgment of America is one that Whitman would have applauded:

> I believe that we are lost here in America, but I believe we shall be found. And this belief, which mounts now to the catharsis of knowledge and conviction, is for me—and I think for all of us—not only our own hope but America's everlasting, living dream.... America and the people in it are deathless, undiscovered, and immortal, and must live.
> I think the true discovery of America is before us.... I think the true discovery of our own democracy is still before us. And I think that all these things are certain as the morning, as inevitable as noon.[39]

These are magnificent words and they express a confidence in man and a faith in democracy and an allegiance to America and its old dream which it is heartening to hear. Who else of all our writers since Whitman has celebrated man and America with a nobler rhetoric and a more inspiriting assurance?

But, as I have already suggested, these sentiments—and I think that Wolfe meant them from the bottom of his heart—are asserted in rhetorical passages rather than exemplified in the episodes of the novel. They come in sections of hortatory prose and are appropriately poetic rather than dramatic in rhythm and in content. The separation between action and idea, which we observed beginning in passages such as the "Unbroken Spinet" rhapsody, is here almost complete. The novelist portrays a dispiriting and despairing world, but the poet-seer lifts his voice to chant the ideal and the promise of America.

Few of us would want to dispense with the dramatic scenes that make *You Can't Go Home Again* a book of truly splendid fragments. And few of us would want to give up the firm assertion of the American dream and possibility which this provincial man kept somehow unsul-

39. Ibid., p. 741.

lied through all his contacts with the depression world. I also suspect that few of us would seriously question that *You Can't Go Home Again* would have been a different and a far better work had it been given Thomas Wolfe to live to find a way of putting the visionary dream and the disillusioning view of man into some harmonious relationship to each other.

Max Lerner has declared that Wolfe's prevailing mood is "the sense of being ravaged and lost, yet finding some . . . assertion of life's meaning." [40] And J. B. Priestley, writing admiringly of Wolfe's position in the great tradition of western literature, declared, "No matter how piercing and appalling his insights, the desolation creeping over his outer world, the lurid lights and shadows of his inner world, the writer must live with hope, work in faith."[41] Though imperfectly, Wolfe shored up hope against the ultimate despair, and fixed our eyes for the moment on distant goals and noble aspirations.

The Discussion

MR. REEVES Do you think that the social criticism in the last novel was increasing at the time of his death, or do you think that he had about said what he had to say on his times?

MR. HOLMAN I would say that it was increasing, and I don't think he had said what he had to say on his times. The awareness of social issues and social problems was steadily increasing, and probably after the summer of

---

40. *America As a Civilization* (New York, 1957), p. 791.
41. *Literature and Western Man* (New York, 1960), p. 440.

1936, his second experience in Berlin, it was a quite intensified reaction to forces he saw in American life that up to this time he had not found necessarily disturbing but that now were very deeply disturbing. Although something like "Boom Town" was written quite early, 1932 or 1933, I think Wolfe was certainly moving closer and closer to a realization of his concern with the outside or the social world, and I don't believe that this trend would have stopped. It is something that people speculate futilely about: what a writer would have been if he had lived when he didn't, but I suspect that if Wolfe were living today (he would be sixty-eight years old) and if he had continued to realize his power and realize it in the direction in which he was working during those last twelve to eighteen months of his active writing, that we would look on him as a quite different kind of novelist from the one we see at the present time. I suspect that *Look Homeward, Angel* might very well be for the career of this quite different sort of novelist an important, interesting, and perhaps by no means best work but one not unrepresentative of his very early career. There is no way in the world, it seems to me, actually to tell what he might have done. If you follow the opposite view that his true subject matter was in fact what he could dredge out of the inner self, the flow of feeling which had to be there before he could write, then perhaps all the signs which point to his being a major social novelist, as I see it, are signs in fact of the dimunition of his talent and his career, and he might never have done anything to equal what had been done. I don't believe this, but it is one very real possibility.

MISS ALDRIDGE   I know this is another paper, but would you like to explore in a very summary manner the implications of the Wolfe-Melville parallel that you suggest?

MR. HOLMAN   I think Wolfe and Melville are writers in many respects very much alike. In the first place, they are alike because both of them are primarily stylists and they write basically in the style of the essayist rather than that of the novelist. Melville is certainly closer to Carlyle than he is to Dickens, and it seems to me that in certain respects we can say the same thing about Wolfe. Another is that there is very little action in the normal sense of action—plot, event—in Melville or in Wolfe—less in Wolfe than there is in Melville; although for a man who wrote what are supposed to be red-blooded adventure stories about the sea, there is an astoundingly small and weak plot line in almost everything that Melville did. Then both of them are likely to locate a kind of protagonist off to one side of the main action and make the art of the story not out of what the protagonist does so much as out of the speculations which run through his mind as he watches events occur. I think this is particularly true of Wolfe in the later books. A character like Ishmael in *Moby-Dick* we almost lose sight of except as a voice commenting upon an action; and if we try to chart the plot of *Moby-Dick* we wind up talking about the nine gams or things of this sort which are, strictly speaking, episodes rather than essential incidents in the plot. I think too that both Wolfe and Melville are what I would call word-intoxicated men—they find it extremely difficult to pass up the opportunity to pry a simple declarative sentence loose and begin inserting things into it. In Melville's case they are often metaphysical conceits, outrageous comparisons of all sorts of things of this kind. Inside a simple sentence are inserted all sorts of levels frequently ranging from the bawdy and comic to the extremely serious. I think Wolfe has the same kind of lack of unity of tone and also the same tendency to explode his sentences and paragraphs and to insert very great wads of material into them. Then, of course, rhetorically they are very much alike. They delight in rhetoric; they are not the slightest bit embarrassed by it or ashamed of it; they are perfectly willing to state what they have to say in rhetorical terms.

MR. COLVERT   If I understood correctly, you were expressing a kind of regret that Wolfe had not found a way to reconcile his rhetorical style to the dramatic style, and I was
thinking in terms of *Moby-Dick.* Would you have the same
regret in that book?

MR. HOLMAN   No, I don't, and I think there is one primary
difference: if *You Can't Go Home Again* were in the first
person, it would have resolved some of these things. The
many different styles and modes of *Moby-Dick* are somehow reconciled and in a sense unified—or justified, if not
unified—by the recurrent sound of the single voice. You
are aware of the narrator; you are aware of Ishmael, re-
gardless of whether he is giving you more information
about whales than you ever wanted or describing a sea
chase or describing his own feelings or brooding in 1851
about the way he feels about what happened in 1837.
There is a personality that is present, speaking. Something
I think happened to Melville in *Pierre,* where you've got
the same sort of mixed styles, but you move to a third-
person narrator, and these styles begin to fly apart; there
is nothing that holds them together. I see nothing wrong
with mixed style. What I was really suggesting to you—
or at least expressing, as you put it, my regret about—
is that it seems to me that in *You Can't Go Home Again*
there is a fundamental ideational conflict between what's
said in these different styles, and this conflict has not been
reconciled. Now the mixed styles exist in *Look Homeward, Angel* and exist triumphantly there. I think we all
accept without any serious question Mr. Walser's reading
of this as a poetic novel carefully woven together. And the
stylistic mix in *Of Time and the River* led Mr. Kennedy
last evening to call it a fictional thesaurus instead of a
novel. It's still unified most of the time, because the materials are unified—the styles are talking about the same

kinds of things. It seems to me in *You Can't Go Home Again* that there really are two different views of the world being put down: one being asserted, one being shown; and that overstates it, but between what's being asserted and what's being shown there is not what I would regard as a necessary correspondence.

Now I think, having said this, we also need immediately to say that we are dealing with a fragmentary manuscript which the author himself had not prepared for publication and which was assembled by an editor who, however skillful he may have been, did not know Wolfe or Wolfe's work very well. He was also confronted with the rather desperate job of trying to salvage some publishable books to get back that $10,000 advance, and he took liberties which I hope none of us would take if we were editing *The Web and the Rock* or particularly *You Can't Go Home Again*. So it is not altogether fair to Wolfe to say it, yet still the basic materials which go into making the book are Wolfe's, and they do express, I think, these essentially unreconciled views of his world.

MR. COLVERT That suggests to me that the specific kind of complexity in Ishmael probably has not been properly studied—that most of the studies on *Moby-Dick* center on Ahab and the complexities of his consciousness, and if in Ishmael you are able to reconcile all these different styles which have a certain implication of meaning, then the implied characterization of Ishmael is indeed very complex.

MR. HOLMAN I think he is, and I think the book *Moby-Dick* has two protagonists, Ahab and Ishmael, and two answers to the questions it sets forth. Ishmael is an extremely complex and interesting person.

MR. DRAKE By this possible drift toward the social novel did you mean to imply—or did I just infer too much from

what was said by other people—that this might have
been a very good thing if he had gotten more social commentary into his novels as he got older and as he became
aware of social conditions?

MR. HOLMAN Would you let me rephrase that and say
that the issue here is a double issue: one is whether or not
Wolfe was moving consciously or unconsciously toward
the outer social world as the subject of his fiction. I
happen to think that he was, and I think there is a fair
amount of evidence that he was doing it or attempting to
do it and that *You Can't Go Home Again* is loaded with
good examples of novelistic scenes, characters, and
actions which are pretty thoroughly centered in the outer
world. "The World That Jack Built" is an example of it;
"I Have a Thing to Tell You" is in large measure an external narrative. As to commentary, I personally would
prefer that he would not make quite as much. Now the
next question (I am separating your question in two parts)
is whether or not I think this is a good thing. I think
whether you think this is a good thing or not is going to
be a function of what you actually want in a novel. Of the
three of us who talked about Wolfe and the novel, I may
be the only one who would say yes, it is a good thing.
I like the social novel, and I believe that this is a proper
medium for fiction; and I think Wolfe might, had he continued the direction that he was moving, have been able
to establish himself very effectively in this medium and
have been a good social novelist, but that is a value judgment. Primarily the issue is what type of novel do you
like.

MR. DRAKE I think so, too, because it seems to me the
more socially conscious the novel the more naive it gets,
because if you compare *The Grapes of Wrath* with *For
Whom the Bell Tolls,* I think the great gulf there is ob-

vious. You don't read *For Whom the Bell Tolls* to get the news from Spain.

MR. KENNEDY I agree with Mr. Holman that *You Can't Go Home Again* is, of all those volumes that are published under Wolfe's name, the poorest. One of the reasons that this is true is perhaps that it is an unfinished work. I wonder if you have ever noticed that it is actually so choppy. What we've got when you look at the amount of pagination taken up by "The House that Jack Built," a little unit by itself, and that European trip with McHarg, and then the long sequence "I Have a Thing to Tell You" is the bulk of *You Can't Go Home Again.* Just these three pieces plus some stuff that Aswell grabbed from here and there and put in, plus parts of the Purdue Speech which he includes, make up the whole book.

There is something else that I think might be said, too, about the social criticism that appears in this book. Surely it is of all Wolfe's works the one which contains the most social criticism because it comes from a particular section of the manuscript that he was writing. Now I would like to relate this to his life to some extent. You may recall that there was a period in which Wolfe felt very much rejected by his publisher and by lawsuits that were being heaped upon him. He left New York City and wasn't going to have anything to do with anything up there any more; and he came down and he rented a cabin in the hills, where he began to write a story or a sequence of the life and times of Joe Doaks. This was all going to be satirical; he was going to start out with Joe Doaks getting on the train, going down to the home territory. He had tried to write this before. He tried to write it in "K 19," and the publisher said, No, don't publish this, and he tried to write it in "Boom Town," and the magazine editor then sliced it to pieces. He tried again, and all this Joe Doaks material was full of satire and social criticism. Later he started to write other things; he began to come back to himself; he began to get more faith in putting together some product; he tied together all that he had written earlier about George Spangler and presently had everything he had written in a long chronological line of material.

The social criticism which appears in You Can't Go Home Again does not reflect, I think, the final period of his writing. One of the last things that he wrote in his life was a good deal of that folk stuff about the Joyners, and remember this had a vivacity, a levity, about it. Also, at the end of his life, he put together some material from "The Hound of Darkness" under the title "So Soon the Morning," and tried to peddle it, and it never did get sold and published—it got shoved in the middle of The Web and the Rock—that part about the promise of America, and the leaves that say, "Promise, Promise." "The Prologue to America" was one of the last things, too. This likewise came out of "The Hound of Darkness." It was the last published piece. Also there is the long piece called "The Promise of America," something that is written about the alter ego's return from Europe and having some faith in America after his return. It appears in his manuscript sequence, I believe, under the heading "Last Poem." Then there is the Purdue Speech, and I think that although he says in that work, that presentation, that he is becoming much more socially conscious—nevertheless this is another piece that reflects affirmation. After all, this is the one in which he says, The people—they are always there; let us never forget that. I think that the social criticism in You Can't Go Home Again—happens to be there, for the most part, because Aswell took the chronological sequence that happened to contain most of this Joe Doaks stuff, and then mixed it in with what he could and made a volume out of it. The result is what we have to be troubled about when we try to discuss

You Can't Go Home Again. But I don't think that it necessarily points the direction of where Wolfe would have
gone. In other words, I am saying there is evidence on the
other side against your own conclusion.

MR. HOLMAN Let me qualify one of the statements that I
have been making. In talking about Wolfe as social novelist I was not consciously talking about Wolfe as a social
protest novelist, but as a novelist whose interest is moving out from the concern with self-expression, with lyrical
self-expression, into a concern with the exterior world;
and in this respect it seems to me that the bulk of the
material that he was writing, including *The Hills Beyond*
section, and things of this kind, also reflect that same
outer concern. I think I quite agree with you that the depth
of the protest which he is expressing in these various
works probably was not a consistent attitude for a man
that was undoubtedly influenced by his feelings about the
world that he lived in. All we have to do is read his letters
to see what a tormented person he was.

MR. DRAKE One can read the novel with some obsessive
preoccupation, but as Randall Stewart said, William Faulkner is not reporting on conditions in Mississippi: he is
reporting on the human condition. Now if people do that,
that is fine, but as soon as they start using the novel to
report the signs of the times and to cash in on the mode
of the moment and the fashion of the hour, then you had
better watch out.

MR. HOLMAN I think I didn't make myself altogether clear.
But I would regard Faulkner as certainly a writer concerned in a very deep way with the pattern and structure
and texture of life around him. All writers, I think, if you
will excuse me, who are worth their salt are selling their
particular view of the universe.

MR. WALSER Ever since I read *The Window of Memory,*
I think the man who is the biggest bane in my life is

Edward Aswell, and it is dreadful because this poor man is in the grave and can't defend himself and no one is coming forward to defend Edward Aswell these days—witness the comments during this symposium. I want to ask you if you think any purpose would be served in a new edition of *You Can't Go Home Again*. If this book is so terribly put together, so wretchedly edited, and we are all ready to believe it—I think so wretchedly edited that it is hardly worth the scholarly introspection that you have given it—would any good purpose be served in getting out a new edition and putting it down there the way Wolfe wrote it and eliminating all these Aswell paraphrases of Wolfe and his own little tidbit substances and so forth?

MR. HOLMAN I have the feeling that we don't quite do Aswell justice. I was trying to suggest this before. Here was a young editor confronted with an enormous stack of manuscripts and with the need to get them publishable and with an outline which is a pretty detailed sketch of where the author had intended to go. I suppose what bothers us about *You Can't Go Home Again* is that what George Webber sees and what happens to him and what he says do not agree.

There are materials that we can ignore in *The Web and the Rock*, and *You Can't Go Home Again*. We could start from scratch, as Aswell did, and whoever does it is going to be confronted with many of the same problems that Aswell was confronted with, and is going to have to make decisions and choices, unless he reprints the entire manuscript, in which case it becomes a scholar's edition and not a reader's edition. You would have three or four different names attached to these same characters; you'd have episodes pieced together out of a number of different fragments; and you'd have the same incidents told several times.

MR. FRED WOLFE I got here a little bit late, but the discussion seems to still center on the uncertainty of *The*

Web and the Rock, and the colossal job which we all admit that Edward Aswell had to do in editing the complete manuscript that Tom turned in to him. Now that job was colossal, and Edward Aswell did it. What I would say is that in New York I was with Mr. Aswell twelve to fifteen times. I would go over and inspect 250 or 350 galley sheets of *The Web and the Rock,* and he disclaimed the fact—which was a glorious fabrication to be forgiven if he had misquoted himself to me—that he did not change one word of the text of either *The Web and the Rock* or *You Can't Go Home Again.* Now he told me that personally time after time, and he went over it with me to make corrections against possible lawsuit. I knew Mr. Aswell well, and I was closely associated with him; I spent time in his home, and when I went to him to take over Tom's affairs, he said he would be honored and glad to do it, and he did a masterful job on it. Edward Aswell had a perfectly colossal job in doing what he and Tom both would have done had Tom lived. I want to change what has been in so many people's minds that Aswell changed too much of that text, and I don't believe Ed Aswell lied to me for one minute—I don't think that he did. On the other hand, Ed might have changed some of the things in that book, and each of you has got the right to his own ideas. But I think his colossal job was in the arrangement and in attempting to safeguard the publishing house and to escape any possibility of lawsuits. Those matters will come up. Now of course I think we ought to give the devil his just due. If Tom had lived, a great deal of it would have been different because both of them together would have done it. Mr. Aswell was a young man just Tom's age—five days difference in their ages—both were born in the same year, the same month—Tom on October the third and Ed Aswell on the ninth, I think. That's all that I have to say, that I do not believe that Ed Aswell was lying, and I personally went over the 250 to 350 galley sheets—not that I could make the corrections, but he would ask the question about what something was, and I would do my best to answer it.

MR. HOLMAN   Thank you, Fred. I don't think any of us intended to question Mr. Aswell's integrity. He certainly had to put together out of an incomplete manuscript the parts that would fit into the outline, and had to make them fit. In fact, I think I had just said before you came in that if we did the job over we would have to do many of the same things that he had done, although we might make different selections.

MR. WOLFE   Anybody that says that Aswell's job was not a colossal job had better think twice.

MR. WALSER   I want to get myself off the hook. I never doubted for a minute that Aswell's job was a colossal job and a very dedicated job. This was the big thing in his life, just as it was in Perkins', as he said. I never doubted the monumental quality of it or the dedication of it, but unfortunately I am a teacher, and you know you can't judge by intention always.

MR. WOLFE   Mr. Walser, if you are over at Chapel Hill— I presented some letters to Chapel Hill, and in those letters was a letter to me from Tom, and the letter reads to this effect. He says, "Dear Fred, I have associated myself with a new young man just exactly my own age—in fact, I am five days older," and he says he believes in him, and Cass Canfield who was the head of Harpers, and they had done something for Tom that had never been done before —made him financially secure. When he signed the contract they had given him a check for $10,000. When he died I talked with the man at Chase National Bank in New York, and Tom had never spent one penny of that $10,000. He had lived on what he had made from short stories. But when he said that this young man believes in me as much as he says he does, and he was going to give up everything else to work with him on the manuscripts of the forthcoming books which happened to be these two, and *The Hills Beyond* that Ed made out of the savings, he said, "I'm going to give them the best job of my life, if it kills me; I'm going to do it."

And this too is at Chapel Hill: "Dear Fred, I have left Charles Scribners and Sons and Max Perkins, and I feel as one mourning for the dead, but I yet feel that I will go back." That is, Perkins first, last, and always was Tom's guiding light, and I think we all know that, and still Tom's guiding light as far as I am concerned—Charles Scribners and Sons.

MR. CORE   I wonder, having gone thus far, if we might speculate on what *You Can't Go Home Again* would have been like if Perkins had been editing it.

MR. HOLMAN   I have been thinking on this, and I think the real problem is that in *You Can't Go Home Again* you are getting pretty far down in the outline which Wolfe left with Aswell when he started the western trip. You are getting down to the point where existing fragments are very incomplete, and it is necessary, if you are going to put them together, to select materials and put them together not in the order necessarily in which they are given in the outline.

MR. KENNEDY   There would be no good purpose served in trying to re-edit *You Can't Go Home Again*. The stuff is in a much cruder state, and there's much more copy. With *The Web and the Rock* it might be an interesting thing to see what could be done, but in the long run it would only serve a scholar's interest, probably. You know all the work that was done on re-editing the *Billy Budd* manuscript, and I regard this as the finest piece of textual criticism that has ever been done in American scholarship, but it doesn't change the *Billy Budd* story as we have known it for years really very much at all, and it would be that way probably here.

MR. HOLMAN I think *You Can't Go Home Again,* particularly the section "The World That Jack Built," is closer actually to the Mark Twain's *Mysterious Stranger* pattern than it is to the *Billy Budd* pattern. You had three different drafts, and the problem was in selecting among them in order to put something together, and there was no conclusion.

I think as far as *You Can't Go Home Again* is concerned, Wolfe always underestimated the amount of time it was going to take him to do something, and he had estimated that it was going to take him an additional six months to get *The Web and the Rock* into publishing shape. This would have meant that, if he had followed a similar pattern in writing the book *You Can't Go Home Again,* this book might have taken two or three more years of work before he had it in a form that was in his own mind satisfactory. I don't believe in this particular context that Perkins could have done much more in editing it than Aswell did. In fact, this is the reason that I said that I thought re-editing it would be primarily to produce a document for scholars who might look at the variant readings or at the varying things, but not a reading text. Somebody has got to make a reading text out of these things, and under the circumstances I think the only thing—and you can't really fault him for it—that bothers us when we work with this book is that Aswell's editing is silent editing, and we have no way of knowing when and how he did it. On the other hand, he was not editing for us; he was editing for his own publishing house and for the estate, and doing it very conscientiously, and trying as best he could to get the best book possible out of this material. If we were turned loose on the book we would probably do many of the same things—perhaps come up with a different book—but I suspect the next generation would attack us for what we had done.

MR. SINGH   When considering the various things, why not consider the varying principles which Aswell seems to have adopted, what was he trying to do, and why was he trying it, and whether it was a legitimate set of guiding principles or not. First, the question of social criticism. Social satire is present in Wolfe's world right from the beginning. Hardly anyone appears in a favorable light, even in his earliest volumes. The reason it is not so prominent there is that Wolfe was more concerned with himself than with the external world. Although it was there, it was not so prominent. If you look at Wolfe's earlier novels there are also a series of disillusionments ending with an affirmation of hope which does not seem to find any justification in the events, but only in the psychology of betterment. I think Aswell probably tried to repeat and to continue the same pattern. I think Aswell tried to do the best job possible in the absence of Tom Wolfe; he tried to do what Wolfe would have done had he not written a single word more. I think he tried to honor the intentions and the general creative pattern of Wolfe.

MR. HOLMAN   I don't—and I think none of the rest of us do—attempt to challenge Aswell's intention or the seriousness with which he tried to carry out the task. The problem that we have—if we have one—with *You Can't Go Home Again* is a problem of the state of the manuscript with which Aswell was working, and the incomplete fragmentary nature of this manuscript. I personally would disagree with you in this respect: I think if I had been editing the book, and I'm rather glad I wasn't, that I would not have included the material from the Purdue Speech in the form in which it was included at the end. A part of our problem is the sudden shift in attitude that comes here, and it comes, I think, from the material that there is no strong manuscript evidence for Wolfe's having intended it to be at that point, though it does complete the book. I would not have moved the farewell to Germany from the end of "I Have a Thing to Tell You" and put it at the end of the novel, because I think it means something radically different at the end of the novel from what it means at the end of "I Have a Thing to Tell You." These are quibbles; they are not major attacks on Aswell; and anyone who edits a body of material as fragmentary as the material that Aswell was dealing with is inevitably going to lay himself open to quibbles and questions of this sort from almost anyone else who looks at this writer or this particular material.

I certainly did not intend anything that is being said about the two different modes or attitudes which seem to me to be present in disparate parts of *You Can't Go Home Again* to be a criticism of Aswell's editing. I could make some criticism of Aswell and I have—not of his intention but how he went about it—but certainly not in this context. I brought him into it entirely in terms that we are dealing here with a fragment, and we are dealing here with a book put together by someone other than the author and without the author's presence.

MR. SINGH   Do you see some parallel between the end of *Look Homeward, Angel* and the conclusion of *The Web and the Rock* on the one side and the concluding chapter of *Of Time and the River* and the last chapter of *You Can't Go Home Again?*

MR. HOLMAN   I see the point that you are trying to make, but I would want to point to what to me is a very great difference. The end of *Look Homeward, Angel* is a personal affirmation, having discovered the self. It is a very Joycean ending; having discovered the secret of art now,

Eugene turns to flee across the now soaring ranges and into the next world. At the end of *Of Time and the River* you have at least a promise—although it is not too well justified in the text—of the fulfillment of love. At the end of *The Web and the Rock* you have the kind of reconciliation of the protagonist to the nature of the world in which he lives—a reconciliation of flesh and spirit takes place. All of these are problems essentially connected with Eugene Gant's or George Webber's coming to some kind of understanding with himself. The conclusion to *You Can't Go Home Again* is not that kind of affirmation. It is addressed to an external world; it is addressed to a social-political situation, and it makes an affirmation about that, not about Webber, and in this respect it seems to me that it is radically different.

Fred W. Wolfe

My Brother Tom

I ought to be scared, but I'm not. I wish that I could im-
plore our Creator using the words used by Tom so often:
"O lost, and by the wind grieved, ghost, come back
again." Oh, if Tom could be here to help his feeble-
minded brother out. I feel like one who hops upon the
horse that they wrote so much about in times gone by and
tries to go four different ways at once. I have no beginning. I'm apt to start in the middle; I'm apt to start at one
end or the other; or open my mouth and just let it come
out and talk. It is my hope and my prayer that something
of what I say might have some value that may stick, or
that what I say might help you.

Now in talking about Tom, you have listened to the
dissection, vivisection, the reassembling, and the putting
together of Tom by some of the most able scholars in the
critical field. They are all friends of mine, but that is not
my field—my field was that of a salesman for forty
years, and I presume that I did talk a little bit in that
profession, so what I simply do is to talk.

I think with our family the two who were most opposite
in temperament all the way through were Tom and myself.
We were a family of eight—five boys and three girls.
My mother was married in January of 1885, and the children then began to arrive. Leslie was her firstborn—ar-

rived in October of that year and died in July of the following year. None of us knew Leslie. She was followed by my older sister Effie, and then by Frank, and then by Mabel, then by the twins Grover and Ben, then myself, and finally Tom in 1900. Now all this is old hat to you, but I think I should mention it just the same.

Tom and I were alike physically to a great degree. Our father was a large man, straight as an arrow—he never had a son who could stand as straight as he did. If he saw a good-looking woman coming into that marble shop of his, that long smock would come off in a hurry, and he would polish those shoes, and he would bow: "Good evening, madam, how are you? Come right in." He loved the ladies, and I think he never had a son who didn't follow in his footsteps.

I was six feet, one and one-half inches at my boyhood maturity; when Tom reached boyhood maturity, why he was six feet, three and one-half inches tall. When he matriculated at the University of North Carolina in 1916, six weeks before his sixteenth birthday, he stood six feet, three and one-half inches tall and weighed but 135 pounds. Through the years he began to develop. At full maturity Tom reached a weight of 235 pounds and a height of six feet, five and one-half inches. I will say this further about Tom: he had big feet—he wore a size thirteen, and about the only place in New York he could get shoes was the Henry Cabot Shoe Store right on the ground floor of the Empire State Building. They had just opened it, and I said, "Tom, I must see it." He said, "Come right on over, and we will take a look at it, but first of all, let me tell you, Fred, that I have found one damn place in New York where I can buy a pair of shoes that will fit me."

Both of us stuttered (I still do, as you will find out), and we both had quite tremendous appetites. Now beyond that, that is the end of the description of two members of the family who are so far apart in other respects. Naturally, Tom had more than a spark of genius.

Now Luke—I am the prototype of Luke in *Look Homeward, Angel* and *Of Time and the River*—stuttered. I went off to Georgia Tech, and Tom tells in *Look Homeward, Angel,* Chapter 10, that Luke worked hard selling the *Saturday Evening Post,* saved his money, and that he did everything that any self-made young man should do to succeed, and he refused to accept help from home, which is true. But he also said Luke did everything but one: "The damn fool wouldn't study." And that was absolutely true. We suffered two distinctions: not only in producing one with a spark of genius and one who was the family fool or clown, but also one who has the very disturbing distinction of being the only ten-year graduate for an undergraduate course—mind you, not for a doctor's degree—that Georgia Tech ever turned out. I entered Georgia Tech in September of 1912, and I finally left there in 1922 with my sheepskin—though I wasn't there constantly.

Now I am not going to take up all of your time talking about the family, and I will answer questions if some of you have them. But I would like to tell something of Tom's early life, as I knew Tom as a boy.

Look Homeward, Angel, his first novel, was the portrait of a young man's life in his early boyhood and his youth. He is painted as being both petted and resented. He was the pampered darling and the ugly duckling, admired and mocked at, and never understood by a single member of his family and his brothers and sisters, except one. That brother was Ben. Ben was the twin brother to Grover; Grover died in his twelfth year at St. Louis in 1904; and Ben died from flu and pneumonia in that terrific attack of flu in 1918, and they both were strangers apart from the rest of us. I didn't understand Tom; I was impatient with him—in fact, I think I was the worst one of the whole family, up to a point, and that point was when Tom was a sophomore at the University of North Carolina in 1917. When he came home that summer I was still laying out orders to him. You know he sold *Saturday Evening Post* for me, and I broke him in upon his paper route—Ben did rather and I went with him. On that particular occasion, I never will forget it, we were walking through the hall, and I said, "Now, you have got to do this and do that." By that time Tom was about six feet, four, and he had come up in weight to about 150 or 160 pounds. He took off his coat, and he said, "Come on out here in this yard. Now you have bossed me ever since the day that I came into this world, and it's going to stop." I said, "Son, do you want to fight?" "If I have to." I said, "You don't have to. Put your coat back on. You are boss from now on." And he was.

Tom was sensitive, and he was very earnest in everything that he did. He even tried athletics, but he was like his brother Fred—he was so gawky and awkward that he couldn't perform satisfactorily at all, but he had a great affinity for reading books. Whenever he wasn't selling *Saturday Evening Post* for me or carrying his newspaper route, you could find Tom in the Pack Memorial Library reading. I think he read everything in that library other than medical journals and lawbooks. He read all my nickel and dime novel weeklies, and I had worlds of them. He read everything.

When Tom was about twelve years old, Professor J. M. Roberts (who is known as John Dorsey Leonard in *Look Homeward, Angel*) was beginning the North State Fitting School, and he prevailed upon Mama to let Tom be one of his students. She said, "Okay, I'll send him for a year." It didn't cost much—maybe a hundred dollars for a year or 125. He continued on until he graduated there and then he entered the University of North Carolina.

Tom was tall for his age and slender—about 140 pounds, and his britches missed his shoe tops by about that high, and his coat sleeves came to here, and with long scraggly hair, the boys led him quite a life for his first term. But that was all—just for the first term. Tom came back after Christmas and as he had found his niche at North Carolina he began to find himself. He was journalistically inclined; he had always been writing little essays and so forth in this little North State Fitting School; but he got into everything, and I think they called upon him too. In succession Tom was either editor or assistant editor of the *Yackety Yack*, the yearbook; *The Tar Baby*, the humor magazine; *The Tar Heel*, the newspaper; and *The Carolina Magazine*. He was a member of a social fraternity, Pi Kappa Phi, and an honorary one, Sigma Upsilon. I think the records of the University of North Carolina prove that Tom was no brilliant student at all, but he didn't flunk: he passed. The only things that Tom excelled in were the things that he was interested in—English, or whatever it happened to be.

In 1918 they prevailed upon the man who had charge of the drama department of the University of North Dakota to come down to the University of North Carolina and take over the folklore plays. He began the Carolina Playmakers. Tom became one of the charter members of the Carolina Playmakers under Frederick Koch, and he put on about four one-act plays. His first was the story of the moonshiner play—"The Return of Buck Gavin." At that time many boys were taking Army training and they couldn't find anybody to act the part of Buck Gavin, so he took that part himself.

When Tom graduated from the University of North Carolina, my mother agreed to finance him for a year at Harvard. Her obvious interest was to get him a master's degree, but that was secondary to Tom. He went to Harvard for three years and in 1922 got his master's degree, but all three years he was under George Pierce Baker, the leading mentor for dramatic students in this country.

Those of you who have studied Tom carefully know what Tom's plan was. Tom's plan was to be epochal—to cover an entire epoch, not to conform to any narrow confines. The result in his plays, *Welcome to Our City* and *Mannerhouse*, was that they would be so long that there would be thirty actors to be fed, there would be nine or ten scenes. The Theatre Guild offered to produce *Welcome to Our City*. They said, "Wolfe, it has great possibilities, and we will produce it, if you will take it back now." And they explained that the play had to be confined to the limit of two hours and twenty minutes and not to exceed four scenes, and instead of thirty or forty actors—a dozen actors. Tom would go back and tear his hair—sure he would fix it. He'd fix it all right. He'd come back—he would have added ten more actors and about four more scenes, so by the time 1924 came around, Tom was a frustrated playwright. A playwright is something like an accordion that you pull out, but you can't bring it back in. But then Tom found his niche.

My mother sent him to Europe in 1924. I was just telling Dr. Reeves about that letter in Miss Nowell's book of letters on page 80. I'm the culprit brother who refused to let him have $500 to extend his stay for four more months. He knew where he was going, and I didn't know it, but he got the money just the same. Tom came back and he took a job teaching at New York University, Washington Square Division, downtown. I'll never forget his first contract: $1750 for nine months. They would hold back about $50 a month and during the vacation Tom would go again on tourist cabin ticket to Europe, supplemented with a little money from home, I suspect. Well, he began to write in the summer of 1926 his first novel. He was in Paris, and he went to London, over to Chelsea, at

Bradbury Street—he took an apartment. He said often at night he would wake up, scratch his head and say what in the hell am I doing here—what am I accomplishing? Well, he would have laundry lists, receipts, lists of people that he had met, he would have everything, and he began to write and put things together and it began to dovetail just like you see a work, a skyscraper go up, and it began to fabricate and take form and shape. The underlying current of his first novel was the fact that there was a deep well of information in Tom's soul, in his heart, that had to come out and it came out—there's no question about that. That was his family and the weather of his own life. He says that he meditated no man's portrait, but of course we know that the portrait was given just the same, particularly in *Look Homeward, Angel.* Tom finished his manuscript in 1928. He peddled it around New York until it was completely dog-eared. I know this because I was there with him at different times. One publisher would take it and then another one—including the greatest book editor of the twentieth century in my estimation, Maxwell Perkins of Charles Scribner's Sons. They all turned it down. Finally Perkins was persuaded to read it, and he wrote Tom that letter in *Editor to Author.* I know you have all read it, and then Tom's reply is in the book of letters. Tom landed in New York on the first day of January 1929. On the second day of January as per appointment he went up Fifth Avenue right past the corner of 47th and 5th, and he said that he was scared to go in, that he didn't know what was going to happen, he was afraid, he was obsessed with doubt and fear as to whether they would take it or wouldn't take it—they hadn't said they would. Anyway he went up on the old elevator to the fifth floor, and an hour and a half later Tom came out like one in a trance, walking on air. He said it was raining. He was clutching in one hand a folded envelope and a folded piece of paper in the other one, and he said that he walked blindly right up Fifth Avenue to the upper end of Central Park, and he looked at them again. One was a contract to publish the novel, and the other was an advance check for $500. He said that up to that time he had never received as much as fifteen cents for anything that he had ever written in his life.

That was where the battle started—the battle between Max Perkins and Tom. Max had that wonderful sense of virtue that so many others do not have. He had the virtue of patience. It took patience to deal with Tom, or Ernest Hemingway, or Scott Fitzgerald, or any of them, but Tom particularly, and Tom knew that too.

How was *Look Homeward, Angel* received? It was Tom's first, written, he said, without rancor or bitterness, but in some respects it was, which he later admitted. We all know that Tom became more objective as he went along. It was received objectively at first and then the fireworks started in Altamont—Asheville. At Asheville, as Tom said, they were reading *Look Homeward, Angel* as if they were reading the pages of the *World Almanac.* He said they saw some things were literally true and that got them to think everything was literally true and literally intended. He began to receive threats, threats against his life—he was told that if he showed his face they wouldn't turn their hands to keep his carcass from being drawn across Pack Square, tarred and feathered. They were all anonymous. Tom was hurt. He had a right to be hurt. In the first edition alone, Asheville absorbed over 1800 copies, and he said that there wasn't fifty people in Asheville at that time capable of understanding why he wrote the book or what he was saying at all. What they were looking for was for the skeleton to be drawn out of the closet. Tom didn't come home for seven years. At that time I was there with him. Well, the same ones who were uproarious to kill him and drag him across Pack Square were the first ones to fall upon his neck, and embrace him and said, "Son, you haven't written anything yet. Wait until we give you what we are going to give you." Well, that wasn't the purpose of writing *Look Homeward, Angel* at all—he wasn't after more information at all. I think that *Look Homeward, Angel* will ever remain, in the words of Margaret Wallace who reviewed it for the *New York Times* on October 27, 1929: "this is a book to be savored slowly and reread, and the final decision upon it, in all probability, rests with another generation than ours." That generation has gone on for forty years. I think that is a little longer than one generation, isn't it? We must be into the next generation, so it is in your hands now, and I think that it will continue to go on.

Tom's second novel, *Of Time and the River*, may not be as popular as *Look Homeward, Angel*, but it carries on where *Look Homeward, Angel* left off. It takes Tom on through Harvard and on to his first trip to Europe and back. But there what will you find? You will find a softening in some respects. Why you will find that he is seeking a little more maturity or objectivity. You will find some of the most soaring passages that Tom ever wrote: his description of trains, his description of his natal month, October—I don't think you need to go much farther than that. Then along came the other two novels—that were published after his death—*The Web and the Rock* and *You Can't Go Home Again*. *The Web and the Rock* is okay—has a lot of good stuff in it, but too much on Aline Bernstein to suit me personally. (And I knew Aline personally and she was one of the darn best cooks that I have ever seen in my life, a wonderful cook, and a wonderful woman and very talented—no question about it.) But I think that when you get into *You Can't Go Home Again*, when you get into Tom's evaluation of America, his love of America,[1] and he gives an equation, a summa-

1. See the conclusion to "The Promise of America," p. 508.

tion of it in his credo which is the final chapter—well you will see that Tom was progressing now. How much he would have progressed beyond the age of thirty-seven years, eleven and one-half months—I'll never be able to tell you. I don't know who will. But personally, I think he would have hit again and kept going; but Tom died, as you know, at the age of thirty-eight.

There's one thing I am going to do and only one. In thirty minutes I can hardly do anything—I'm just getting warmed up, but I want to read here something that I think is one of the greatest things that Tom ever wrote, and I will tell you why I think it is one of the greatest things he ever wrote. I got him the stationery from the office of Providence Hospital in Seattle, Washington. This wonderful letter came for me from Max Perkins addressed to Tom. He said, now Fred, you will know whether Tom is well enough to receive it. I gave it to Tom. His eyes lighted up. He said, "Fred, get me the stationery. I'm going to answer that." It was against orders; he wasn't supposed to do it. But this was the last thing in life that Tom Wolfe ever wrote, that letter to Max Perkins on August 12, 1938. I was at the foot of the bed. I handed Tom magazines to write on, and he would look up with his quizzical eyes and he knew I didn't know what he was writing. This remarkable letter was the last thing Tom ever wrote.[2]

I would like to conclude with Tom's own words: "... a stone, a leaf, an unfound door; of a stone, a leaf, a door. And of all the forgotten faces. . . . Remembering speechlessly we seek the great forgotten language, the lost lane-end into heaven, a stone, a leaf, an unfound door. Where? When? O lost, and by the wind grieved, ghost, come back again."

2. See Elizabeth Nowell, *The Letters of Thomas Wolfe* (New York, 1956), pp. 777-778.

Ladell Payne

Thomas Wolfe and the Theatre

MR. PAYNE   There are at least two or three different questions we might consider as we discuss the importance of Wolfe's dramatic training. One of these is, of course, what was it that Wolfe learned at North Carolina and at Harvard? What were Professors Frederick Koch and George Pierce Baker teaching? Another is what is inherent within the novels themselves that is in some way related to the drama, either related specifically to what Wolfe had been taught or, beyond that, to the whole question of the genre—of whether or not Wolfe was indeed using techniques borrowed from the drama? And the third question, which is more interesting to me than the first two, is to what extent did Wolfe use subject matter, subject materials, in these plays which he later used in a different fashion in his novels?

Claude W. LaSalle II in "Thomas Wolfe: The Dramatic Apprenticeship" argues that Fred Koch always emphasized four major concerns in his teaching at Chapel Hill. One of these was the constantly reiterated doctrine that you should write about what you know. We know that Wolfe subscribed to this even though he did not practice it when he wrote "Buck Gavin" and some of the other plays for Koch at North Carolina; but at least the doctrine was clear: Write about what you know. And I suppose the relationship is reasonably self-evident once you get into the novels.

Second, Koch emphasized the accurate depiction of realistic environments, and this emphasis is obviously reflected in Wolfe's novels as well as in his plays.

Third, Koch was refreshingly aware of social problems at a time when American literature was relatively unconcerned with such matters and, in fact, when there was pressure against seriously treating some social issues in novels and plays. LaSalle argues that the impetus in Wolfe, particularly that which becomes evident in the last novels, toward dealing with social problems could well have been a result of his contact with Koch.

Finally, LaSalle contends that Wolfe's total career shows that he was influenced unfortunately by Koch's concept of the proper approach to art. Koch seems to have argued over and over again that form was not of primary or secondary or even tertiary importance, but a matter to be considered somewhere further down the line; the all-important concern was the subject matter. The main thing was to say what was important to you, to say this as enthusiastically as you could, and to let form come along the best way it could.

In discussing George Pierce Baker at Harvard, Mr. LaSalle points to Baker's emphasis on technical excellence, on writing salable or performable plays; he recalls that Baker's great purpose was to develop producing dramatists who could go to Broadway and become Eugene O'Neills. And as we know, Baker repeatedly tried to get Wolfe to make his plays more performable, to rework his materials. In short, Baker was in many ways an earlier Maxwell Perkins.

Baker's emphasis on form and Koch's emphasis on content bring us directly to one of the ways we can approach this discussion of the impact of Wolfe's dramatic training upon his fiction.

Mr. Walser This morning I did not bring up this point in my paper because I was working at other angles and from other views, but when I was writing the paper, I kept thinking about Professor Koch, and I believe that I am the only person in this room who ever knew him and had a class under him. Poor Professor Koch had me one semester, and he thought that everybody could write, and he proved that he was wrong with me, because he never could do anything with me. But the fact that he did so much with so many other people was a remarkable thing. "Proff" Koch was not a genius. You had it pretty well: he had several points that he kept pushing home. One of them was that everybody could write—he had me believing that I could—I couldn't, you know, but he had me believing I could; and he kept saying to us— this class—"Don't seek for themes in the North Pole or in Europe; look at your own hometown." You see where I'm getting. "Look there, look in your own backyard. There is drama. There are people. There are wonderful events. There is life. There is character. Look there, and don't worry what's happening in New York or Paris or Tokyo or whatever exotic spot you might choose to write your play about." And the people of course did this. I wrote a play about Lexington, this town I grew up in. It was awful; I've got it today. Professor Koch gave me an A+ on it, and the reason he did was that he wanted to keep telling me that I could write a play, which wasn't true—I couldn't write a play. He said look home. I don't think it can be proved that when Wolfe got around to choosing a title for his first novel, choosing his thematic material, he was thinking about Professor Koch saying day after day, "The play is in your backyard, look at your hometown, look at the people there, look for the plot there." I can't prove it, but anyway that is a possibility.

MR. PAYNE   Of course, the truth is that when Wolfe started writing "The Return of Buck Gavin: The Tragedy of a Mountain Outlaw" (I have always felt that "tragedy" in this case should be pronounced "travesty") he was not following this particular dictum.

MR. WALSER   He didn't in his plays, but did later when he began to write prose fiction—I wonder if all of this came back, maybe not consciously, but was just in his blood. It was in the blood of all of the students growing up at Chapel Hill in those days who were dealing with Professor Koch. And this string of writers that Professor Koch produced is impressive from Wolfe to Paul Green and dozens of others.

I think there is another relationship between the content of the plays and the novels as well. I would like to talk about what within the novels seems to be dramatic.

MR. GEORGE REEVES   It seems to me that one very evident result of the playwriting experience is Wolfe's ear; he learned to listen for dialogue; and one finds this not only in *Look Homeward, Angel* but also finds it in the vignettes or montages that he did in the later novels. When George Webber was abroad, he was able to hear a line of dialogue sitting in a cafe in Paris, and this sort of thing. A great many of these little one-line things, and sometimes a long conversation, ring very true; and it seems to me that this "Gentlemen of the Press" which we heard here today was a good example of how real and live his dialogue can be—the words seem to come straight from life. But it also seems to me that he did not acquire discipline from his dramatic experience, the kind of tightness which a dramatist must get. In fact, I think when he gave it up and began writing freely, which he wanted to do all the time, by reaction he went to extremes in the other direction.

MR. PAYNE   The thrust of what you are saying seems to point toward an innate talent that enabled Wolfe to reproduce what he saw and what he heard. What about the *techniques* he used to create characters and scenes? Do they come from what he had learned about creating characters for the stage? How much of his work in constructing a fictional episode comes about as a result of what he had done in working for the stage?

MR. SINGH   I think it is not often remembered that Wolfe almost made Broadway. I think what made him feel that he had the stuff in him was his later sense of conflict and tension. If you compare his works with steam-of-consciousness novels, especially *Ulysses,* his hero is always in conflict with social and human knowledge, and this can be seen in various episodes. These little things are more or less one-act plays, in themselves. What contributed to his disillusionment with the medium? He wanted to explain this conflict, and I think that is probably why he made the right decision to stop playwriting and change to the novel. But the fact of his training and the fact that he had the dramatic instinct in imagining and creating a situation fraught with tension and conflict have been beneficial to his novels.

MR. PAYNE   Frequently we have a novelist whose characters are engaged in tension who emphasizes the internal struggle of the mind and resolves these conflicts through the thinking process.

MR. SINGH   I am talking about tension between characters. That is really dramatic tension which you can see on the stage very much more clearly than any conflict in the mind.

MR. PAYNE   What about the creation of characters? What about the way they are put together?

MR. SINGH   Yesterday the distinction was made between flat characters and round characters, and Wolfe offered an instance in writing when this kind of terminology breaks down. In "The Party at Jack's," in the same chapter he presents over two dozen characters, each summed up in just half a paragraph, sometimes less than a sentence. And yet all of these people are summed up in a phrase, and they are not flat because Wolfe has not taken up some characteristics saying this is a man: he is getting to the roots of the character.

MR. DRAKE   Sometimes things get flat, or can be flat on purpose. I should think one of the most outstanding examples would be the catalogue of guests at the Jacks' party, which I might say is one of the things that William Styron lifted bodily into his first novel, which I think is one of the most brilliant pieces of writing in the last decade, and it is this marvelous little thing that Fitzgerald does— he matches reputation with names—Stonewall Jackson Abrams of Georgia—that is all you need to say about those people. You have them, as it were, before you. I don't think you are really contradicting Forster there— it is flatness with purpose, flatness with meaning. And I would like to ask Mr. Walser this: Do you think that Professor Koch's advice was so very bad?

MR. WALSER   I certainly do not. I think all the proof I would need that it is very good advice would be to point out the roster of well-known people in his class.

MR. DRAKE   I think it was great, and I tell all students that for three years he studied at the best place he could. I think inspiration helped to propel him, and it certainly helped him to capture what Mr. Singh is talking about in "The Party at Jack's" and the various other instances that the dramatic is interspersed throughout all his fiction writing.

MISS ALDRIDGE   I would like to go back to dramatic structure and a statement that Mr. Singh made—that Wolfe wanted to explain more than he wanted to represent. Had Wolfe aspired to, or wanted to, represent a little more than he wanted to explain, might he have succeeded as a dramatist?

MR. KENNEDY   Your question is so broad that one might say what one started to say even before you asked it. I have three points that I would like to toss out. It seems to me that what Wolfe learned mostly at Harvard (though he got started a little at North Carolina) was a talent for presenting a scene. If you notice the plays that Wolfe wrote, he will have some very interesting scenes, he will begin to develop characters, he will begin to arrange some kind of conflict, but then when he goes to the next scene he will do much better if he can produce a couple more characters and if he has them talk about something else. He doesn't seem to be able to progress, to develop a particular plot in the usual way, which indicates that he should have been another kind of playwright, but at any rate he had a talent for scenes, and he got an opportunity to exercise this very well. He is better at a one-act play than he is at a long play; he is better in *Welcome to Our City* than he is in his three-act plays because *Welcome to Our City* is made up of ten scenes, each one of which has a different set of characters for the most part.

How does this show up in his novels? It doesn't show up quite so much in *Look Homeward, Angel* because that novel is written in a way that has a good deal more of what Phyllis Bentley calls summary rather than scene. Material will be developed not by means of dialogue over a stretch of several pages, but through a little dialogue, a little summary, a little more dialogue, a little more summary, then some kind of poetic flight on the part of the narrator, and so on. When he comes to write *Of Time and the River,* he is able to develop scenes much more fully in that book; and one result is that that book turns out to be very much longer than the others. There is still the same kind of problem: the scenes don't really go anywhere; they develop a certain kind of character or conflict of characters which he can meditate on, brood on, react to, or something of that sort.

I would like to say, secondly, that I don't know what it is that makes for a successful playwright beyond being able to produce what directors and producers are willing to put on the stage. You've got to get the material on the stage or you are nothing as a playwright. One of the things, of course, that was true in Wolfe's time is that the kind of craftsmanship which would develop a particular plot was much more demanded then than now. When his play *Welcome to Our City* was produced at Harvard, it was thought of as a very revolutionary play; it was thought of as kind of expressionistic, as a matter of fact. If you look closely at parts of it, you will notice that it has stylized kinds of behavior which will be presented on the stage from time to time, and that there is effective montage, particularly in the opening scene of the play.

What Mr. Singh reminds me of is this problem of craftsmanship that Wolfe had, beyond his ability to put together a series of vignettes like *Welcome to Our City* that were to some extent held together by a kind of associative method, rather than one that follows the principle of probability. But he almost got a production. What is remarkable is that he was told by Lawrence Langner, one of the most powerful men in the theatre, that if he would cut a half hour out of that play, he could get it put on, and Wolfe actually could not do it. Dick Walser could have done it. He says he is not a writer, but he could have cut that play, if Lawrence Langner had told him he would put it on for him. I have talked with a friend of Wolfe's —a man who was in the Harvard workshop with him—a man named Henry Carlton. He said that Wolfe went up to his summer place in New Hampshire right after that, and Carlton said they would talk at night about what could be cut out of the play, and then he, his wife, and family would all go to bed, and Wolfe would stay up and work on the play; and in the morning he would have added to it. This is one part of the problem.

The other part of the problem is something that Aline Bernstein has pointed out. She is a person who worked in the theatre for years. She said Wolfe never would have been successful in the theatre because in the theatre you have to cooperate with other people, and he was such an individualist that he could never cooperate with other people: everything had to be done just his way. In the theatre there are electricians, stage hands, technicians that have to have something done in a certain way, and the playwright has to make a little change to see that it can be carried out that way, but Wolfe could never do this sort of thing; and this is another reason he never succeeded in the theatre.

But the third point that I would like to make is that I think he could have had some kind of opportunity to get a piece produced if he had had somebody to do some work on it with him—a kind of play doctor like George Kauffman. Kauffman used to work with all kinds of people, helping them get their novels into drama, and helping them work out their autobiographies in drama, or whatever. Wolfe's piece would have been an expressionistic play, or a play made up of a series of scenes. If he had developed a reputation or lived on a number of years later, he would probably—because he had this dogged kind of determination—have, at some point in his career, said, All right, now I am going to show them that I really can do this, and he possibly would have with the help of somebody else.

Toward the end of his life, when he was in Asheville for the summer, he was very, very upset about the way his summer was going and his writing was going, and he was in town away from that mountain cabin that he stayed in, and he got terribly, terribly drunk. He got so drunk that he was arrested and put in jail for disorderly conduct, and while he was in jail at the police station, a policeman went to Hubert Hayes and told Hayes that Thomas Wolfe was in jail and would he like to come down and talk to him. So Hubert Hayes went to the jail and talked to Wolfe. Wolfe was sobering up, and Hubert Hayes was a playwright, so Wolfe started talking about plays, and he told Hayes that he would have given everything that he had ever done if he could have had a successful production on the stage.

MR. REEVES   And, of course, the irony of that was the staging of *Look Homeward, Angel,* which won a Pulitzer Prize and the New York Drama Critics Award.

MR. PAYNE   Mr. Holman would you like to respond to the question?

MR. HOLMAN   Yes, I think Miss Aldridge's question is a good one, because it seems to me that it gets to one of the real problems in Wolfe as a writer. The question dealt with the conflict in Wolfe between representation and commentary, and she was asking whether, if Wolfe had been able or content to present his characters and action in dramatic form, he would have been a better novelist. I think that this does get at an issue in Wolfe because we remember over and over and over again Wolfe as a writer of scenes, characters, and actions that are vividly realized in the world of senses and in the world of dialogue; and a tremendous amount, it seems to me, of what lingers in our memory after we have read Wolfe is not his writing at all, but the key gestures that exist. For example, in the death of Gant there are a whole series of very simple gestures which are almost stage gestures, that express both the long loneliness and the bridging of the loneliness between Eliza and W. O. at the period of his death—very moving, and moving in a quite different way from rhetorical statement. But I think Wolfe was never willing to let these things stand alone, or perhaps he didn't trust us enough, or perhaps there was for him something that was overriding as far as the dramatic scene was concerned. He always had to find a means of reinforcing it, of talking about it, to be certain that we understood it the way that he understood it; and, therefore, there was a heavy weight of rhetorical explanation which got into his work. These are likely to be the phrases that we remember, the sentences and the paragraphs that we remember out of his works. And I think this thrust was so strong and so basically a part of him that despite all of his best efforts that he never would have produced a successful play unless someone forcefully sent him to Siberia while he wrote it.

I would like also to make a comment on "Proff" Koch and the 47 Workshop situation. It seems to me that one of the things which Koch taught Wolfe in addition to confidence in himself and the belief that he was a young genius—and this is important to beginning writers—was also self-indulgence, which I think was also characteristic of Koch's method of teaching. It was a thoroughly undisciplined kind of writing, and we can see that if we look at "The Return of Buck Gavin," which the Playmakers are going to do at Carolina in about ten days as a part of their celebration. It was on the first bill of the Playmakers, and they are going to repeat it. I've been looking at what it really is. He wrote "Buck Gavin" in three hours—early morning hours before an assignment was due, and took it in and read it from an almost indecipherable manuscript, and this is the way it appears. There are some letters—one in particular—that I am sure you remember that he wrote Koch when Koch wanted to reprint "The Return of Buck Gavin" in the *Carolina Folk Plays,* second series. Wolfe was protesting its being reprinted and then, too, he was almost bitter about Koch's not having taught him that writing is a disciplined craft and that it is hard work. I think the thing that he learned at Harvard that was so valuable to him—and it certainly shows up if you compare "The Third Night" or "The Return of Buck Gavin" with *Welcome to Our City* or *The Mountains* or some of the other work that he did later— was craftsmanship, the ability to handle a scene, to make a scene work on the stage and to work with it until it was a successful dramatic representation, and it is an invaluable attribute for any novelist to be able to envision scenes and be able to describe them in terms of action and dialogue. But I cannot really believe that he ever could have conquered his unwillingness to leave to us the interpretation of the world that he was describing sufficiently to have allowed us to see his play even as a part of expressionism.

MR. WALSER   I agree with you, but you balance things on scales—maybe Koch was indulgent, but maybe that lack of indulgence was balanced off pretty well in the confidence that he tried to give Wolfe and everybody.

MR. PAYNE   Before we adjourn I would like to make a couple of comments. First, I think the point made about characterization is valid. That is, it strikes me that Wolfe does indeed use the Ben Jonson kind of character, the Dickens kind of character, the character who comes on stage with a tag line, a stutter, or a visual gesture. But

Wolfe's caricatures somehow seem more credibly human than most of Dickens's people. For, while a Dickens' figure frequently has an abstractly symbolic dimension, a Wolfe caricature usually takes on the kind of psychological complexity commonly associated with so-called round characters. Uncle Bascom Pentland is the kind of character who illustrates the point I am trying to make here.

Finally, it should be noted that some of the characters, motifs, and situations that Wolfe first created for his plays appear full-blown in his novels. In *Welcome to Our City* he depicts the sexually vital Essie Corpening, a character who will appear only slightly changed later on in *Look Homeward, Angel*. In this same play there is a conversation between a father and a son about how the father and son are going to get along, how they are going to establish some sort of communication between themselves. It strikes me that there is an obvious concern here with the kind of struggle for human communication that Wolfe later explores in *Look Homeward, Angel*.

In *Mannerhouse* Wolfe has a character named Eugene talking with his mother. Eugene says, "Long, long ago, dear Mother, I wandered out of Arcady. And never may I find the path that takes me back again" [p. 40]. This motif of the lost way first stated in this play becomes, as Professor Walser's paper clearly demonstrates, the dominant theme of *Look Homeward, Angel*. I would argue, in short, that in addition to whatever other effects Wolfe's dramatic training had on his work as a fictionalist, writing plays gave him the opportunity to introduce themes, characters, situations, and issues he would explore fully later on in his novels.

Paschal Reeves

New Directions
in Wolfe Scholarship

MR. REEVES   To begin I would like to read something on
The Letters of Thomas Wolfe to his Mother. This is from
Scholarly Books in America (October 1968). Carey Bynum
picks the books that he likes and comments on them,
and as you know Professor Holman and Miss Ross have
newly edited from the original manuscript these letters
to his mother. Mr. Bynum has a number of things to say
but I want to read just this part of his comments.

> For Thomas Wolfe, it is difficult to conjecture a might-
> have-been. This Southerner, in the life he had, probably
> produced the definitive prose work for the 20th century
> and there seems little hope of anyone usurping that posi-
> tion. Still, he need not have gone beyond the thirties. His
> portion of the era set the guidons to be carried through to
> the end. In a special sense, his life was the child of this
> century, begun in its first year and finished far short of the
> mid-point; it was raw substance for the times, a traditional-
> ist core immersed in the alchemy of transition.
> In the last decade, there has been a rather paradoxical
> trend in the Wolfe chronicle. More people, it seems to me,
> are reading books about Wolfe than are reading books by
> him. They are interested in his behavior within the scope
> of the forces at work during those times. And though the
> biographies have done much to clarify this behavior (the
> recent Turnbull biography as a case in point) we still get
> the subjective view which can be misleading.

And he goes on to praise the edition very highly. The point I want to make here is that we often get the subjective view, which can be misleading. For the past thirty years Wolfe criticism has been biographically and autobiographically oriented, and it is fascinating to each new reader as he comes to the Wolfe canon, but it seems to me that now is the time for the serious students of Wolfe to launch out in new directions, and we would like to hear what some of these new directions are.

MISS ALDRIDGE A few years ago Mr. Holman made an observation to the effect that the most pressing need at the time in Wolfe scholarship was for a study of Wolfe's novels in the light of romantic critical theory. I believe that was before Mr. Kennedy's book. I wonder if he feels that book satisfied the need, laid the groundwork, opened the field. I would like for him to address himself to that and then I'd like to hear from Mr. Kennedy.

MR. HOLMAN I think that is still a primary need for Wolfe, because it seems to me that in many respects Wolfe's aesthetic is essentially the same as that of the nineteenth-century English romantic. I don't believe that this was in fact what Mr. Kennedy was attempting to do in his study of the literary career, particularly as it is reflected in the manuscript remains, although there is an enormous amount in *The Window of Memory* which contributes to this theory, particularly the clear indications that run through that book of Platonic and Neoplatonic ideas as they begin to show up in Wolfe, the emphasis on John Livingston Lowes's theory of the imagination and Wolfe's response to this — all these seem to me to be significant contributions toward a study of Wolfe in terms of the romantic aesthetic. I think perhaps, Mr. Kennedy, you would agree that you were not trying to make that kind of study, and perhaps that study needs still to be made. In fact, I think it does, because it seems to me that really this is the way Wolfe thought about art and the way Wolfe responded to the world and the problem of incorporating the world in some kind of permanent artistic form.

MR. KENNEDY The way I would answer the question is to say that in *A Bibliographical Guide to the Study of Southern Literature* I made some remarks about the state of Wolfe scholarship today, and some things that I thought perhaps should be looked into in the future, and I said that one of the things that I felt should be considered with care was Wolfe's relationship to the romantic poets. I didn't put it in connection with theory—aesthetic theory. One can do this in connection with aesthetic theory. Since Wolfe is not a theorizing kind of person, the scholar or critic should have to create the theory in some ways out of what he found in Wolfe's scattered remarks—except for one document that Wolfe left which is the opening section of his unpublished work called "Passage to England," where you have the speaker discoursing about the question of the imagination.

MR. HUTTON Perhaps the way to get down to the nub of this is to ask the four of them—Professors Holman, Kennedy, Walser, and Reeves—what they intend to work on or what they are working on as far as Thomas Wolfe is concerned these days—not necesarily what they think is important, but what they are (laughter) ...

MR. WALSER I would like to do a book called something like Undergraduate Tom Wolfe or Tom Wolfe (not Thomas) at Chapel Hill—just the way Mr. Kennedy did the Harvard years, but not as thoroughly as I would want to do the Chapel Hill book. I would love to do this for several reasons. In the first place I was graduated at Chapel Hill in 1929, and Chapel Hill was still sort of the same place then that it was when Wolfe was there. I knew so many of the people who were actors in it.

I don't know that I ever will do the book. But it seems to me it ought to be done because Chapel Hill in those days was a very vibrant place, and I feel that this would help to explain what happened to the young fellow when he was there.

MR. KENNEDY I say now that I am not going to do anything on Thomas Wolfe any more, and I have said that at times in the past. What happens is that I have my note cards too upon which I have jotted something, and I have even outlined some material, and then something will happen and I'll say to myself, You know, I really ought to do that; I ought to go ahead and do thus and so and after that I will not do any more on Thomas Wolfe. So this is the way it goes. I have put together part of an edition of the correspondence of Elizabeth Nowell and Thomas Wolfe, and the only thing that I have got left to do is the part that does not involve any work—I've got the text, and I just haven't done the footnotes and introduction and that sort of thing; and I would include as a kind of appendix a couple of versions of a long piece that Wolfe left unpublished at the time of his death with which Miss Nowell was closely involved, as an illustration of some of the kinds of ways they worked together. That piece is "No More Rivers."

I also wrote a chapter on Thomas Wolfe at NYU as a teacher, and then special circumstances that I won't go into at the moment forced me to take the chapter out of the book that I wrote, so I have got it and I have always wanted to amplify it and publish it as an article. One of the things that I have long been interested in doing, and if I don't do it, I will help some graduate student of mine get involved in it, and that is try to put together that piece "K 19" that Perkins wouldn't let Wolfe publish. It is there in evidence in Wolfe's papers, and I think from the kind of paper that Wolfe used, pagination, and so forth, that this could be picked up here and there from the Wolfe material and put back together again. I myself would like to see whether Perkins was justified in persuading Wolfe not to publish that. You see the projects that I have been talking about have to do with research and editing and that sort of thing. I apparently like to work this way. There are critical topics, topics that deal with ideas of one sort or another that I will be glad to suggest to my graduate students or to you, but I don't think I would do them myself.

MR. HOLMAN   I think we shouldn't leave Mr. Kennedy and Mr. Reeves without mentioning that they have completed a work you have not yet seen, a really magnificient edition of the pocket notebooks of Thomas Wolfe, which will be published in two volumes. If Mr. Kennedy sounds a wee bit weary on the subject it is understandable after having labored as long and faithfully and well as he has with Mr. Reeves in getting together this really remarkable collection of timely data that all of us are going to have to depend on in a major way for almost anything that we do with Thomas Wolfe from this point on.

As far as I am concerned, I think I am a little bit like Mr. Kennedy. I always resolve with whatever I do about Thomas Wolfe that this is the last time and that I am going to turn to something else and probably not do anything else with him. I still hold that resolution. I've written some fifteen or sixteen separate essays, many of them overlapping in ideas, in which I have said about everything that I have to say about Thomas Wolfe, and what I am doing at the present time is putting these essays together. I realized when I looked these essays over that there was one work of his which I had in large measure ignored. It's *The Web and the Rock,* and I suppose eventually I will get around to trying to deal with that novel in a little more detail than I have before. As far as major work is concerned, I have no plans. I have all kinds of respect for those who are reading Thomas Wolfe's hand and editing, but having worked with the letters to his mother, I don't believe I am going to join that august company again.

MR. REEVES   I understand all these sentiments, and I share them. Years ago I set out to write a master's thesis, and I selected as my title "Race, Nationality, and Class in Thomas Wolfe." I thought that had some substance to it. I visualized three chapters: one on race, one on nationality, and one on class. The thesis turned out to be just the Negro in Wolfe, so I have been plowing that field for a long time, and I finally got out of my system the race and nationality in *Thomas Wolfe's Albatross,* and I still want to do class. There are some things in the Wisdom collection that I would like to edit, but what I want to do first is an edition of plays. I still think they ought to be collected in one cover, and I plan to do that, and I have done some preliminary work on it.

MR. MARSHALL   Mr. Walser, has anyone ever studied folklore motifs as reflected in stories about Thomas Wolfe himself?

MR. WALSER   About him—no.

MR. MARSHALL   You mentioned apocryphal stories—and that few could be documented. It seems to me that you could study folklore motifs and these stories about him and try to find out which ones were true and which were apocryphal and why they were—why they arose.

MR. WALSER   The elements of folklore in Wolfe have been argued for time. The sort of thing that I had in mind was the hundreds of roommates that Wolfe had at Chapel Hill.

MR. LINER   I would like to ask about the possibilities of working with Wolfe's humor and particularly his satire.

MR. WALSER   Professor McElderry at Southern California and Mr. Reeves have both written on this. I am interested in the humor of Thomas Wolfe, because one day I want to do a book of North Carolina humor.

MR. HOLMAN   I think there is a strong and frequently unrecognized strain of humor in Wolfe that is both comic exaggeration and a kind of distancing which he attempts to make as he looks at his younger self—where he uses a whole series of comic devices, not with the greatest grace and finesse in the world, but certainly well enough to establish by and large what he's doing. Then from the beginning on there was, as Mr. Singh pointed out last night, a substantial amount of social criticism in the form of social satire, and I have always had a feeling, without actually exploring it in any way, that from the early twenties on, Sinclair Lewis, particularly in the period between *Main Street* and *Dodsworth,* was a major influence on Wolfe's attitude in some of his matter. This has been kind of known casually I think, and I don't know whether there is enough in it to be worthy of extended examination, but I think it is part of the Wolfe method. We find, too, in this respect that Wolfe is working in a tradition very much like the T. S. Stribling tradition—most of us are very happy to forget this I think. They are talking about much the same kind of people located in sections of the same mountains, and there is a good deal of the same type of humorous exaggeration involved in representation of characters in the earlier Stribling books before the trilogy and in what Wolfe was doing in *Look Homeward, Angel,* particularly. Both were trying to describe life in the mountains and in a mountain town.

MR. CORE   Was Wolfe trying to exorcize the demon, you think, when he wrote *You Can't Go Home Again*, in that passage about Lewis—trying to get away from that particular pattern?

MR. HOLMAN   I never thought of it that way. I don't regard the Lloyd McHarg section of *You Can't Go Home Again* as humorous. I think it is one of the most pathetic things that Wolfe ever wrote, and I think it was pathetic to him. He felt it very deeply, because this was the experience of the man who had in a sense welcomed him publicly on an international scale to the brotherhood of major writers and could bestow fame with a few words in Stockholm. Then Wolfe meets him and finds that fame itself is such an empty thing. I think this happens with most writers and certainly with Wolfe—he sees here a reflection of himself and a possible warning that makes it not an effort to exorcize the Lewis influence so much as simply the awareness of the emptiness of fame and the tragedy of a man like this. I never felt that the section was funny.

MR. WALSER   I was very impressed recently by a review essay in the first issue of the new *Southern Literary Journal* by John William Corrington that the time had come when all of us who are interested in Wolfe had to stop wrangling about the old Wolfe problems that have concerned critics and writers for so long, particularly the failures in certain areas, his pack of faults, we want to get rid of that autobiographical content, the lyric quality of first novels and so on. That all these Wolfe may have failed in, but the time had come when we had to stop talking about these, and he used Dickens—he said Dickens had faults, faults all over the board, but every time one begins to write and think critically about Dickens you don't have to go through all that wash again, and I liked the way Corrington said it. I had never seen it put quite this way, but I suppose it had been thrashing about in my mind for a long time. And what Wolfe seems to need then is no more of this. There are the failures, there are the faults, just as Dickens had them, just as all great writers had them I am sure, but let's get on with what we have and try to discover the values and the virtues and the truths which are there and forget what he didn't have.

MRS. BUTLER I would like to ask Mr. Holman about the question he raised last night of social awareness on the part of Thomas Wolfe. I wonder if you don't find a good many of the things in *Of Time and the River* have a social awareness. The river people, for instance—the Pierces and their set.

MR. HOLMAN Yes, I would not want to suggest that Wolfe's social awareness in the sense in which I was talking about it last night began with the latter part of *The Web and the Rock* and *You Can't Go Home Again;* it is present in Wolfe all the time. I think that it tends to develop in his own responses to people as he moves out into a new world and looks at this world in a different way than he had looked at it back at home. I think though there is a quite different quality in the attitude he is taking toward the Pierces, for example, in *Of Time and the River* and the Jacks in *You Can't Go Home Again.* He is fascinated by the Pierces, but finally he does reject their way of life: it is not for him; but there is a long and very detailed and rather admiring portrait of these people and their way of life until at last he sees that he cannot fit into it. There's a quite different basis I think for "The World that Jack Built," and it is much more directly a criticism of the system than the first is. The first is still very much a personal reaction, and the latter seems to have found some sort of social frame, social attitude. I think the whole University of Utilities Culture business that Abe Jones is in is again a part of his own response: it is his attempt to find himself in relation to his students and his work, and it is on the whole less sympathetic with the people with whom he is dealing. The distance between him and Abe Jones, though he is finally able to bridge it to an appreciable extent, begins by being a very great distance indeed, and he seems to feel that they live in different worlds. By the time he gets to *You Can't Go Home Again* there is a much closer identification of himself with the people of the world like Abe Jones. So I think that the change is gradual; that it is a development on Wolfe's part of some kind of identification with, an appreciation for, an attempt to grapple with the problems of an external world much less personally and less centered within his own emotional response than it is in *Of Time and the River*. So that essentially the outer world becomes the subject in *You Can't Go Home Again* in a way in which it is not the subject in *Of Time and the River*.

Mr. CLAYTON   I would like to go on with this just a bit to *The Hills Beyond*. We haven't discussed this very much. As we know, *The Hills Beyond* was the original novel that he had planned on his forebears for *The Hills Beyond Pentland,* and he had a lot of material on this but he used it up, he said, in the two novels after *Of Time and the River,* and then he started on a new novel of ancestry, and according to Aswell this was the last work that he was doing—he was writing and rewriting this. I would like to ask Mr. Holman, since he has been discussing this, if he considers that this novel was becoming more of a vehicle for social context than his other works. In this short work, this abbreviated history, Wolfe the author repeatedly although obliquely, intruded to continue to make comments on such things as pseudo-aristocratic organizations, the crude life style of mountaineers, the inequities of law and justice, and lawyers, and the evil of civil war, also symbolized by old Looky Thar, and he hangs on to life causes of past traditions.

Mr. HOLMAN   I think there are two things we could comment on, actually. This attempt to write the earlier history of the family is not a late thing but a very early one. In a sense this is the way he wound up before he pitched the first ball, and so, to a certain extent, he repeated this material over a period of time. I think the primary difference that we have in the use of these materials in the fragment of *The Hills Beyond* is a difference in tone and matter, and here he does seem quite consciously to have adopted a manner and tone which is fundamentally that of the folk humorist, the teller of tall tales, which he had done sporadically before but not as a common device. Mr. Reeves has dealt with this as one of the characteristics of his work; I remember hearing him give a very fine paper on it. Here again, I think, we are dealing with a segment of material where Wolfe is interested in looking at a world and trying to describe it and finding a means or way of describing it and he is attempting to do it differently from the way he attempted to do this in, say *Of Time and the River.* But I also think the kind of social criticism that he is making of the South in its social and political history is not new to this period of his life. It shows up in his early plays: he said much these same things. He got almost in essence the same attitude toward the social institutions of the Old South expressed in *You Can't Go Home Again,* in one passage where he talked about America having lost its way, sometime after the Civil War. Then in *The Web and the Rock* he imagines a figure who goes into the woods to the house that's in the woods and gets lost, and it takes a long long time to find his way out again. Quite obviously he is using a symbol to describe ancestral worshipping and inward turnings in the South, whose social institutions are not in contact with the larger world. I don't think the attitude that he is expressing is relatively new, and one of the real debates is whether or not he really succeeds in telling the story effectively through the use of a kind of folk humor as his basic voice. I think Mr. Reeves thinks he does.

MR. REEVES   I happen to disagree with my colleague Mr. Kennedy on the value of this prose material, perhaps because I am too steeped in the tradition of the Old Southwest humor. We must remember that *The Hills Beyond* is a very different book than Wolfe intended in *The Hills Beyond Pentland,* or even as he was shaping the course, but I think he succeeds very well. What Wolfe was doing here was that he was coming back home, and he had always had big ears and had soaked up this material in boyhood—this oral tradition—and that he was certainly employing it in his characterization. I don't think he expected to raise his characters to archetypal stature, but that he certainly thought of them as representative of a bygone era, and that he could comment on his own times through them. He was becoming more acutely interested in society. As I see it, he progressed from a solipsist, from an egocentric individual into an author who was interested in society and in the forces shaping it, and he saw these materials of the ancestral voices of George Webber as shaping his milieu. I agree with Mr. Holman that this was the new mode for him perhaps—another mode but not a new attitude. I think the attitude had been sort of sleeping along very early— in *Welcome to Our City*—I think it was there in embryonic form. I am very sorry that he didn't finish this book—I would like to have read a number of things that he projected.

MR. CLAYTON   Just one idea—it is a short work, it is a fragment, but in that fragment, he managed to get an awful lot of comment on social ideas, and I just wonder if his work was becoming a big social commentary. He was doing more and more of this.

MR. KENNEDY   Mr. Clayton, a moment ago you had a number of points that you made. I think these are sufficiently significant observations on the social criticism that we find there. They are worth stating in some longer form than you put them in just now. I have never really looked at the book quite that way before, and I think you ought to do something with these ideas.

MISS ALDRIDGE I thought last night we left *You Can't Go Home Again* in rather bloodied shape. Are there reasons that we might go back and read *You Can't Go Home Again* and *The Web and the Rock*?

MR. HOLMAN I think one of the reasons for going back to *You Can't Go Home Again* is that it contains a very large amount of Wolfe's very best writing, if we want to look at Wolfe as writing about an exterior world rather than about himself. Certainly two sections of it represent materials about as well organized and as clearly expressed and as adequately controlled as he ever did. One is "The World That Jack Built"—Mr. Kennedy and I differ about whether the long or short version is the better one— but whichever version you read, this is remarkably effective and remarkably controlled and in the long version in *You Can't Go Home Again* it is 200 pages and virtually a novel in itself. "I Have A Thing To Tell You" is another extremely well controlled novella; and there are other individual incidents that are superb. Katamoto is one of my favorite people, and I would hate to lose him or the material about Boom Town; the Federal Weight, Scales and Computing Company seems to me to be a little heavy-handed, but on the whole very effective satire; and the Lloyd McHarg section works for me extremely well. Now all of these seem to me entirely justifiable reasons for being glad we have this book, and for reading it and rereading it, and I think what we were probably doing to the book at my instigation last night was talking about it in terms of the attempt that was made to give it an apparent unity and organization by taking these successful elements and trying to sandwich them into a running narrative which really didn't exist in anything like a complete form.

If I had to take *The Web and the Rock* or *You Can't Go Home Again* there would be no hesitation on my part in taking *You Can't Go Home Again,* despite the fact that there are sections of *The Web and the Rock* which are really magnificent. Again they are sections. I think this is true of Wolfe all the way, even in *Look Homeward, Angel.* Wolfe wrote in terms of sections and segments of work which are reasonably self-contained and which come off very well and frequently are tied together with materials that are less successful than the material which precedes it and follows it. This is more obvious it seems to me in *You Can't Go Home Again* than it is in the earlier works— largely because *You Can't Go Home Again* in my opinion has shifted its emphasis away from a narrator or a protagonist whose personal emotional involvement can justify the inclusion of this great accumulation of things, and therefore the very objectivity or relative objectivity and external quality of the materials in these excellent passages make the very imperfect scaffolding by which they are put together more obvious than it is in the other books, because this scaffolding too deals with the external world.

Mr. Payne   Are you saying, then, that a man who wrote long novels succeeds most in the short sections?

Mr. Holman   I think I would almost say that he is not really a novelist, and that is really the problem that we have with dealing with Wolfe—that he isn't a novelist and almost any of these definitions that we impose upon him exert upon his work demands which in a sense it isn't fair to ask, because this is not really what he was meaning to do.

MR. KENNEDY   You were asking about this specific volume that was published under Thomas Wolfe's name. I speak of it this way because I think of it as a part of a larger sequence. Mr. Clayton was talking about this novel or this partial novel, *The Hills Beyond*. I think of it as part of a longer sequence, and I can only see a value in *The Hills Beyond* as part of this longer sequence. I cannot see a value in it by itself. And I feel to some extent that way about *You Can't Go Home Again* because of the kind of thing that I was saying last night—that it is largely made up of three big chunks, each of which has its own integrity, but the rest of it is made up of sprinklings.

MR. CLAYTON   Is that integrity sufficient for us to study?

MR. KENNEDY   I do not think the work is worth studying as a whole. Once I had a class read *You Can't Go Home Again*—I will never do it again. I have had classes study *The Web and the Rock;* I have had classes study novels other than *You Can't Go Home Again* and have had great success. I tried those two sections Mr. Holman took out of *Of Time and the River* once, and that didn't work— the whole thing wasn't there. My idea of what is of value there in *You Can't Go Home Again* is what one might find, let's say, in the whole "Party at Jack's," if we could take it out and put it in an anthology called Great Short Novels of American Writers or something like that. I think it is difficult to try to put it into that sequence. I am sorry that I feel that this long work of Wolfe's that I try to see altogether (and I am referring to the whole long manuscript that he left behind) has to end with this choppiness. But that's all we have, so that is the way I look at it. I am amazed to discover what different tastes Mr. Holman and I have when we agree on many other essentials. He really does like a novelist who deals with the social scene —I prefer the novelist who looks inward. This is why I like *The Web and the Rock* a great deal more; it is a far richer book with so many more fully developed units within it that can be fitted together, but it has got some of that same problem that *You Can't Go Home Again* has.

MISS GREEN I would like to ask Mr. Kennedy if he foresees any eventual publication of the correspondence with Aline Bernstein or is there an injunction against this? It might prove a fascinating biographical corollary to *The Web and the Rock* or even *The Journey Down.*

MR. KENNEDY What I know about this is about the same thing that some of the other gentlemen know: namely that Mrs. Bernstein didn't want this correspondence published in her lifetime, and that Edward Aswell was trying in her last days to persuade her to edit it, but she did not. Her heirs so far have not wanted it to be published, though they allowed Andrew Turnbull to publish some letters in his biography. I think the time will come; I hope the time will come when someone can persuade Mrs. Bernstein's daughter or maybe her granddaughter, who has just been graduated from Bryn Mawr, to edit it because they have so much more information about who some of these people are that she has mentioned in connection with the theater. She herself led a very interesting life, not only within her association with Thomas Wolfe, but in her association with so many people in the theater; and in the earlier part of her life her association with some people in the world of art, with George Bellows and with Robert Henri, the American realist. Every now and then I say to a group of my graduate students that I think there is a wonderful subject in a biography of Aline Bernstein, if they want to try to do this sometime. But a person who will do it should be a woman, and I think that person should be Jewish, because such a biographer could bring a great deal of special understanding to Mrs. Bernstein's life—more, certainly, than I could even though I know a great deal about her. At any rate, the state of the Wolfe-

Bernstein correspondence right now is that it is restricted; it is in the Harvard Library; nobody can look at it. Paschal Reeves and I were allowed to examine it in connection with our editorial work on the *Notebooks,* and I think he would agree with me that it is a fascinating correspondence, although Mrs. Bernstein tends to say the same things over and over again. There are no special secrets of any sort—it is just a revelation of a kind of interrelationship that is personal, and for this reason Mrs. Bernstein didn't want it published during her husband's lifetime. If her husband had died before she did, I feel sure she would have edited the letters.

Mr. Walser All the secrets were revealed about Mrs. Bernstein and Wolfe. Now what is the real reason that the heirs don't want that correspondence to be published? Is it the old feeling of Mrs. Bernstein's that she didn't want it done?

Mr. Kennedy It is her private life. She was willing to treat it in fictional terms—project herself, and this seems odd to us, but after all, they were her letters and she did not . . .

Miss Aldridge But did she indicate specifically that they would be published after her death? She didn't want them published during her lifetime.

Mr. Kennedy Of course I don't know the answer to that question, but even though she said that to somebody, once the right to publish passes into the hands of her heirs, then the decision is someone else's. Her immortality is associated in many ways with those letters and she knew it. That is why she gave Wolfe's letters to the Harvard library.

Mr. Reeves I think at this point we should recognize Mr. Singh and ask him if he will pull these diverse threads together for us.

MR. SINGH   I think the development of ideas in Wolfe is marked by a logical progression almost as close-knit as from enunciation to demonstration in a Euclidian theorem. Wolfe begins by questioning the place of man in the universe of time and space. His concept of time is progressively evolved from his view of a single moment— a complex, transitional point in the ever-flowing river of time, pressed down by the accumulated impact of the past and aquiver with the hopes and misgivings of an unrealized future. The Wolfean moment has roots deep down in the past and has also the promise of fully realizing in the future life, seen as growth and development, blossoming and fruition, thus takes its character from the single moment of which it is composed—the moments which have the seeds of the future planted in the past. The raison d'etre for Wolfe's obsessive attempts at recreation of the past is his desire to trace this cycle of growth. His thought goes from the past through the present into the future in a search for certitude about life, its nature and purpose.

Loneliness is one of the principal themes throughout Wolfe's writings. It is not only the theme social isolation of an individual but a cosmic vision of the essential loneliness of man and the confrontation of man with his universe, not of the individual with society. Wolfe's characters are seen as lonely persons because they lack communication with others, and their bewilderment and insignificance is viewed against the background of the illimitable space of the universe in which they are lost. It is because of this perspective in Wolfe that his statements about loneliness often include a reference to the vastness of space. Thus, in the dimension of space, man is an insignificant atom in the infinite universe while in the dimension of time he has a transient existence in the eternal universe. In Wolfe's ideas about time and loneliness, there is a significant parallelism which gives a coherence and a central unity to Wolfe's image of man. The development in his novels is from a tormented awarness of the brevity and littleness of the individual's life in the dimension of time and space to the reassuring knowledge that human life endures from generation to generation and that progress is a historical fact.

The spirit of the individual, beset by mortality and loneliness, and seeking self-fulfillment in the infinite and eternal universe—this is the essential theme of Thomas Wolfe. And although Wolfe insists upon the grandeur and glory of the spirit, there is little proximity in his ideas to the theological notion of the immortality of the soul. Wolfe's idea of the spirit does deviate from the mundane and the secular. Even when he ascribes, in a rhetorical fashion, immortality to man, he defines its origin as love of earthy life and not the theological emanation from a supreme Godhead. The journey of the protagonist-hero is from an anguished awareness of his isolation and the tragic brevity of his life to a certainty that mankind's march ahead is not interrupted by ephemerality of individual existence and that a wider social concern is the antidote for loneliness.

The tenuous form of Wolfe's novels springs from his basic theme; the movement or action in his novels is reminiscent of, but not coequal with, the form of the picaresque novel. The development of his style reflects the same progression from a self-centered individualism to participation of an individual in the life around him. The language of the earlier novels is intensely poetic, rhetorical and sometimes descends into downright rant. But in the later novels when the protagonist-hero is interested in the world around him, there is a sober objectivity, a relaxing of emotion, which is in marked contrast to his earlier style. There is an intimate relationship between Wolfe's metaphysics and his technique of characterization. In accordance with Wolfe's concept of time as a river in whose on-rushing waters men are caught like inexpert swimmers, his characters always appear in a state of involuntary mobility. The so-called "giantism" of Wolfe's characters has been the subject of considerable adverse criticism. The aesthetic necessity for adopting a larger-than-life scale arises, once again, from the themes of Thomas Wolfe and the nature of the conflict in which his characters are engaged. On a stage where a remote, imperturbable time and an immense limitless space are among the principal actors or at least never absent from the consciousness of the human players, the latter must be given an amplitude and extension in keeping with the proportions of the drama. But as Wolfe progressed from the concept of human life hedged in by mortality and isolation in the dimensions of time and space to the idea of individual existence merging in the wider life of mankind, his characters also shed their gargantuanism.

I am afraid I could not give evidence in support of all these wild assertations, because that would take a lot of time, but I am sure that you all could recall what particular chapter or characters or incidents that I had in mind.

Mr. Reeves   Thank you very much, Mr. Singh. We appreciate your summation. Let me extend my appreciation to these gentlemen who have read papers, to Mr. Payne for his discussion, and to all of you for your participation in this symposium. It has been a pleasure to have you as our guests here at the University of Georgia.

List of Participants

Joanne Aldridge
Lorraine Anchors

Jack M. Beasley
Beverly Beckham
Wayne E. Bell
William H. Bonner
Mrs. William H. Bonner
Mary Carol Boserup
Tyus Butler
Mrs. Tyus Butler

Nan C. Carpenter
Mrs. Robert Carson
Austin Catts
Julian Cave
Mrs. Julian Cave
James B. Colvert
George Core
Mrs. George Core
Michael Clayton
David Clements

Joseph K. Davis
Thomas Davis
Robert Drake

Elizabeth Evans

Barbara Fitzgerald
Randolph Fitzgerald

Charmian Green
John C. Guilds

C. L. Hardy
Susan Hatfield
Fay E. Head
Sandra Helsley
Mary Ann Hickman
John Hiers
Mrs. John Hiers
Janice Hill
C. Hugh Holman
Lawrence Huff
John Hutton

Betty J. Irwin

Gerald Kahan
Richard S. Kennedy

Thomas Liner
Jane Litton
Stanley Longman

George O. Marshall, Jr.
R. M. McCommons
Mrs. R. M. McCommons
Luetta Milledge
Rayburn S. Moore

George Niketas
Michael Norins

James J. Owen

Eugene F. Parker
Sarah Paulk
Ladell Payne
Bernon Peacock
Joan Phillips
Mrs. W. R. Potts

Gay M. Rapley
George Reeves
Paschal Reeves
Mrs. Paschal Reeves

Larry M. Sams
Mary Sanders
Mrs. C. L. Shelby

Andrea Shipley
Hari Singh
Mrs. Hari Singh
Mrs. Carter Smisson
Jo R. Smith
Norwood Smith
Hazel Jo Smithco
Julia Stanley
Sara Strickland

William R. Thurman
Mrs. A. D. Thurston

Jimmy Voyles
Ninh Thuy Vu

Kenneth E. Walker
L. H. Walker
Richard Walser
Leland Warren
Mrs. Leland Warren
Nancy Weed
Robert H. West
William J. Wolak
Fred Wolfe
Mrs. Fred Wolfe

Letter from Thomas Wolfe
to Mrs. William E. Dodd

One of the highlights of Wolfe's life was his triumphal visit to Berlin in 1935. The American Ambassador, William E. Dodd, and his wife, their daughter Martha, and their son Bill, all received Wolfe most cordially and extended him many kindnesses. Just before he left Berlin, Wolfe wrote Mrs. Dodd the following letter.

Berlin
Thursday, June 13, 1935

Dear Mrs. Dodd:

Before I go away I want to write you these few lines to tell you again how grateful I am to all of you for the wonderful and generous kindness and hospitality you have shown me during the time I have been here. I have never known anything like it—the usual experience of a stranger in a strange city is so different—this last month in Berlin has been one of the pleasantest and happiest times I have ever known in Europe. If I have stayed so long and said goodbye to you so many times the reason was that it became harder all the time to leave a life and friends that had been so magically and unexpectedly discovered. Now it seems to me I have known you all for years: I cannot believe I came to Berlin just a month ago, leaving here now comes as a real and painful wrench. I shall never forget how Martha gave up almost all her time to me this last month—I know how many friends she has here, how many parties, meetings and excursions she has given up on my account and if ever the chance comes to reciprocate, in whatever way I can, I will do it with all my heart. Martha has become my friend, and now I want her greatest success and happiness and achievement as if it were my own, and if there is ever any way of my helping her towards it, the chance to give such help would bring me the greatest joy.

Finally, I want to tell you how proud it has made me to have known you and Mr. Dodd. You are the first Ambassadors I have ever known, I don't know what the rest of them are like, but it is a wonderful thing to know that people like yourselves have been sent here to represent America in a foreign country. For the country's sake, naturally, I hope you may stay here a long time, but for my own it makes me a little sad to think I may not see you until years have passed. I hope that doesn't happen—I may have to come the whole way back to Berlin to keep it from happening—anyway. I'm not going to say good-bye now —I am just going to send you and Mr. Dodd and Bill and Martha all of my best and warmest wishes, my most grateful thanks—

Sincerely,

Tom Wolfe

Index

University of North Carolina, 42, 74, 114, 117, 123, 138
Untermeyer, Louis, 33

Wallace, Margaret, 121
Walser, Richard, 99, 107, 130, 135
Warren, Robert Penn, 5, 89
Web and The Rock, The, 2, 11, 30, 33, 36, 41, 100-112 passim, 121, 140-151 passim
"Web of Earth, The," 10
Welcome to Our City: 118, 129, 130, 134, 135, 147
Wharton, Edith, *The Age of Innocence*, 32
Whitman, Walt: 43, 90, 95; *Song of Myself*, 8, 29
Wilder, Thornton: *Our Town*, 38
Wilson, Edmund, 87
Wolfe, Benjamin Harrison, 14, 115, 116
Wolfe, Effie (Mrs. Fred W. Gambrell), 114
Wolfe, Frank C., 114
Wolfe, Fred W., 7, 77, 107, 114, 116
Wolfe, Grover Cleveland, 114, 115
Wolfe, Julia Elizabeth (Westall), 113, 116, 117, 118
Wolfe, Leslie, 113
Wolfe, Mabel (Mrs. Ralph H. Wheaton), 114
Wolfe, William Oliver, 114
Woolf, Virginia, 6
Wordsworth, William: 11, 48, 49, 50, 51, 71, 73, 74, 75; *The Prelude*, 8
"World That Jack Built, The," 83, 85, 101, 109, 144, 148

You Can't Go Home Again, 5, 13, 82-112 passim, 121, 142-151 passim